Textured
Bead Embroidery

Learn to make inspired pins, pendants, earrings, and more

Linda Landy

KALMBACH BOOKS

Kalmbach Books
21027 Crossroads Circle
Waukesha, Wisconsin 53186
www.Kalmbach.com/Books

Lettered step-by-step photos by the author. All other photography © 2014 Kalmbach Books except where otherwise noted.

The jewelry designs in *Textured Bead Embroidery* are the copyrighted property of the author, and they may not be taught or sold without permission. Please use them for your education and personal enjoyment only.

Published in 2014
18 17 16 15 14   1 2 3 4 5

Manufactured in China

ISBN: 978-1-62700-044-4
EISBN: 978-1-62700-185-4

Library of Congress Control Number: 2014940828

Editor: Erica Swanson
Art Director: Carole Ross
Technical Editor: Jane Danley Cruz
Photographers: William Zuback, James Forbes

Contents

FOREWORD

I met Linda Landy years ago in a classroom setting. I immediately noticed this lady had something different about her. She was a great student, full of questions and very, very busy at her table. She took the classes seriously, not only taking in the technical instruction but the creative process.

Then like an explosion and with a huge grin on her face, Linda presented her own crazy, wonderful ways of doing her own "thing." I wanted to stick her in my pocket, take her home, and be inspired by her design sense and unconventional approaches to the craft.

Linda marches to her own beat which is nothing short of fabulous. Her designs are all her own. In my observation, she's classy with a touch of off-the-wall craziness, allowing her uniqueness to shine through and making her stand apart from the crowd!

I am honored to call Linda Landy my friend. She is not only a gifted artist and perfectionist in her craft, but a caring beautiful individual who shares what she knows and is a wonderful human being.

Sherry Serafini

Take a Spin Cuff
by Linda Landy

INTRODUCTION

There is a very predictable reaction when I show someone my work for the first time. Their eyes get real big and they ask, "How long did that take?" Really? That's what they want to know?

I remember the first time I saw bead embroidery. My mother had dragged me over to Sherry Serafini's table at a Bead&Button Show Meet the Teachers. It was the first B&B for me and for Sherry, and I fell in love with the medium. I never asked how long it took. I wanted to know how to do it! Over the next few years I took classes with Sherry at every opportunity, but I found every class incredibly frustrating and unproductive. I simply could not reproduce her style of work. The beads didn't lay right. I couldn't stand seeing the foundation through the beads even when it was dyed. My beads didn't want to follow her graceful curves. My work puckered and curled.

Finally, I started a collar with a cabochon I had found on vacation in Maine. When I looked at it, I saw a beach at sunset and decided that I would let the cab dictate the flow of the piece. I struggled at first, but finally gave in and let the beads take over. I had no idea what I was doing, but all of a sudden it was working. I was clustering some beads and using others in uncommon orientations. I liked what I saw, and textured bead embroidery was born. I've described my work as "Sherry Serafini on steroids," but it really is much more than that.

This book will teach you the techniques you need to create bead-embroidered works that are sculptural, three-dimensional, and very textured. We will talk about the design concepts of flow, balance, color, and theme. In addition to basic stitches, there is a bead-by-bead guide to textured bead embroidery and 12 step-by-step projects to inspire you to get started. This book also includes a CD of patterns for the projects so you can simply print and begin.

Bead embroidery is one of the most liberating forms of beadwork. There are few rules and boundless opportunities. There are really only a few simple stitches, and "changes" are incredibly easy. You'll be surprised just how quick and easy it is to create spectacular one-of-a-kind bead embroidered bracelets, necklaces, pendants, earrings, purses, and art pieces.

On the other hand, bead embroidery is not like the paint-by-number projects we did as children. The beauty of bead embroidery is the freedom of the work. Use your imagination to create your own unique design. You can always just thread a needle, sew up through the foundation, and let the beads do their thing.

Linda Landy

Basics

   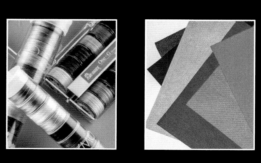 

Gearing Up

If you have experimented with bead weaving or bead embroidery, you probably have most of the fundamental tools and supplies you need to get started. Of course, there just might be that one tool that you can't live without...

MATERIALS

Needles

Beading needles come in several sizes. The most common are 10, 11, 12, 13, and 15 (the larger the size number, the smaller the needle). A size 12 needle is considered to be the most versatile—it can be used with 11° round and cylinder seed beads, most 15° seed beads, and any bead that is larger. Use a size 13 or 15 for smaller beads.

Traditional beading needles are very flexible and thin, and usually about 2 in. (5cm) long. Although these needles are fine for bead embroidery, some beaders prefer "Sharps" needles, which have round eyes, medium lengths, and sharp points. Sharps are not actually any sharper than other needles, but they are shorter and usually stiffer. Use the needle that you are most comfortable with—one that is relatively easy to thread and that will pass through a bead several times.

If you work with any kind of leather product, your hands will appreciate Glovers needles, which are sharp triangular pointed needles used for piercing leather. Glovers are available curved or straight in a variety of sizes.

While these needles are flexible, they do break and bend, so always have an extra pack on hand. Never force a needle. Popular needles include John James and the newer Tulip needles.

How to thread a beading needle

Threading a beading needle is one of the hardest things for beginners to learn. The truth is that you never thread the needle; you needle the thread.

Unwind a length of thread, and use it in the same direction as it comes off the spool. Trim the end to remove stray fibers, then moisten and flatten it. Hold the thread as close to the end as possible, with very little thread showing between your thumb and index finger (barely enough to see). Limiting the amount of thread sticking out past thumb and finger keeps the thread stiffer and discourages the thread from sagging or splitting. Examine the needle's eye to find out which side has the wider opening, and push the eye over the thread and down between your fingers. With a little practice, this method makes threading a needle considerably less frustrating.

FOUNDATIONS AND BACKINGS

Bead embroidery can be done on a number of foundations. Until recently, one product dominated the market, and you could purchase beading foundation in any color that you liked—as long as it was white. If you wanted any other color, you had to dye it. Today, there are many options available in tons of colors. Here are some I have tried:

Lacy's Stiff Stuff

The most popular medium for bead embroidery, Lacy's Stiff Stuff is a smooth beading foundation appropriate for small, delicate pieces that can also hold substantial weight. It will hold its shape and is washable and dyeable. It is available in white 4¼x5½ in. or 11x8½ in.

CPE EZ Stiffened Felt

This is regular craft felt that's been stiffened into sturdy sheets. Kunin Foss Stiffened Friendly Felt is available in more than a dozen colors in 9x12-in., 9x18-in., and 12x18-in. sheets.

Nicole's BeadBacking

This firm felt blend is stiff enough for textured bead embroidery, but supple enough to give your work a nice drape. It resists fraying more than some of the others. It is available in 14 colors and two sheet sizes: 12x9 in. or 9x6 in.

Beadsmith's Beading Foundation

The newest product in the field, this foundation is advertised as stiff and durable, easy to bead through, washable, shrink-resistant, and dyeable. It is available in black or white in either 4¼x5½ in. or 8½x11 in.

Bead enforcement

This stabilizing material for bead embroidery projects is distributed exclusively by Knot Just Beads. It is stiffer and thicker than Lacy's and holds up better to tighter, denser work. The polyester/rayon-blend fabric is washable and available in 4x5-in. or 8x10-in. sheets.

Ultrasuede

Many bead artists work directly on **Ultrasuede** or soft leather. Ultrasuede fabric is a durable, yet soft, backing for beadwork. Ultrasuede is cruelty-free and easy to wash, and it doesn't wrinkle. It is made from synthetic micro-fiber. I use it more as a backing than as a foundation. Some of the thinner Ultrasuede fabrics will stretch, so test it before you use it.

Embossed felt

I love texture, so it's no surprise that I fell in love with **Kunin/Foss Embossed Felt**. Made of Eco-Fi polyester from recycled post-consumer plastic bottles, it is slightly stiffer than wool felt and fade-resistant, and it cuts cleanly with no fraying. It is available in 12x9-in. sheets in several patterns and colors. I use it as a backing.

Fish leather

You can also try **fish leather**. The textures and color choices are amazing—and it really is fish skin (without the fishy smell). The eco-friendly and chrome-free tilapia leather skin is vegetable tanned and naturally dyed by hand. Choose suede or glossy in fabulous colors like rust, moss, green, natural, turquoise, fuchsia, and purple. Due to the natural origin of the material, there are significant variations in size, color, and texture. It is surprisingly tough to sew through—try a Glovers needle— and the back tends to fray and pill if you bead directly onto it. Just trim the fuzz with scissors as needed.

THREAD

There are many threads on the market that can be used for beading. Some beaders swear by a thread that others refuse to use. For years, beaders primarily used two threads that were originally manufactured for the upholstery industry. As interest in bead weaving has skyrocketed, a number of new products have been introduced. These are a few that I currently use for bead embroidery. Try them out to see which one works for you.

Nymo

Nymo is one of the earliest beading threads and is still in widespread use. The nylon beading thread is soft and strong, and it will not create large holes in the bead embroidery foundation. It comes in a wide variety of colors and thicknesses to accommodate most beads. Size D, especially strong and versatile, is the most commonly used and available thread. It is the only size I recommend for bead embroidery.

C-Lon

This beading thread is advertised to not need conditioning or stretching. It offers the drape and ease of Nymo but with more durability. C-Lon comes in 36 delicious colors. It does not stretch, which can be a problem when you are working in certain applications like peyote stitch using cylinder beads; however, it also has a tendency to fray.

Fireline

Fireline is a strong, flexible, heavy-duty bead thread with little or no stretch. Originally developed for fishermen, it is stiffer than nylon thread but the smaller sizes (4-lb. and 6-lb. test) will fit though the eye of a #12 beading needle. Fireline has a textured but slippery surface, which can sometimes create tension problems and make it difficult to knot securely. Spools of Fireline will display

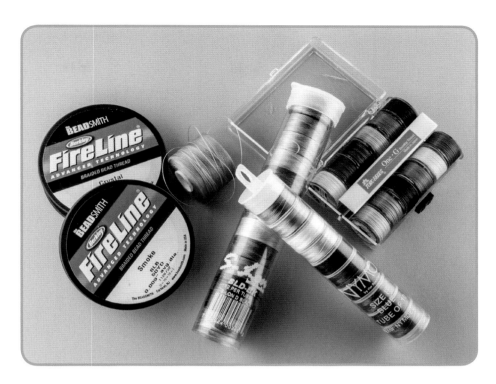

two numbers. Focus on the test strength. The most popular sizes for beaders are the 4-lb., 6-lb., and 8-lb. test. My favorite is 8-lb., and I use 10-lb. for metal beads and crystals. It is available from the manufacturer in smoke grey and crystal, and sparklespot.com sells 6-lb. test colored Fireline with an after-market coating in 16 colors.

Toho One-G

This beading thread is a very silky smooth nylon thread with a beautiful drape, available in 12 colors. Slightly thicker than size B Nymo, it is easy to thread and can be used in all bead-weaving applications. If you avoid working with long lengths of thread, you should have no troubles with fraying.

Thread color

You will be surprised how the color of your thread affects your finished work. Black thread is dark and shows through most beads. This can be an advantage if you like the shadow of the thread to set off your colors. White thread is best suited for white or extremely light-colored beads. Neutral colors such as taupe, tan, beige, and gray work with a lot of bead colors. Keep in mind that the color of your thread can enhance, change, or completely gray out transparent or translucent beads.

When using several bead colors at the same time (and to limit the unpreventable exposed thread from showing), use a dark neutral. A dark thread may show through pale beads, but as a rule of thumb, a darker color will show less than a lighter color. When possible, match your thread to the beads. When finishing bead embroidery, matching your thread to the backing makes a big difference in the appearance of your work.

Thread length

I hate to add new thread, so I work with the longest length possible. Unfortunately, the longer the thread, the more likely it is to tangle—which isn't much fun, either. So you have to find out what works best for you. I find that the longest length of thread I can handle is the span of my arms.

TOOLS

While everybody has their own preferences, these are the tools I find essential for comfortable beadwork.

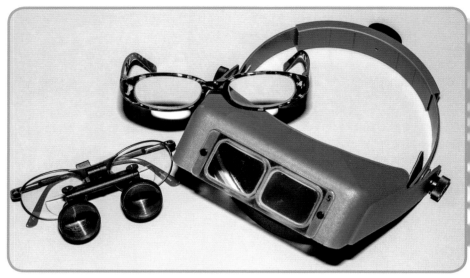

Scissors

You will need needlework scissors for cutting threads. Choose a pair with slender blades and sharp points to allow precise thread cutting. My favorite is the 3½-in. embroidery scissors that look like a stork. I also keep 5-in. knife-edge craft scissors in my toolbox for finishing my pieces.

Bead tray

While there are many choices available today, my favorite is the BeadSmith Bead Mat Tray. The lightweight, durable 11x14-in. tray has a ½-in. lip. I line it with the coordinating removable soft, foam-like mat which keeps beads from rolling. If you are willing to invest a little more, the Bead On It Board has a unique board surface. If you shimmy the board or run your fingers over the top of the beads, they will all settle hole-side up. It has oversized padded edges to keep the beads on the tray, and rounded corners to prevent you from catching your beading thread. The board is weighted and the bottom is skid resistant.

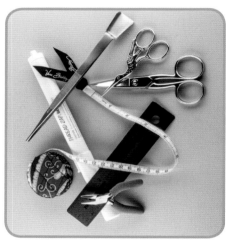

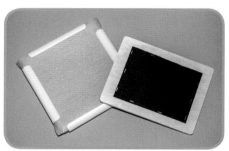

Task lamp

I can't emphasize enough how important it is to have proper lighting for beading. Several companies manufacture craft lighting—specially formulated to show colors accurately and details clearly with low heat, low glare, and illumination—in everything from a portable travel lamp to a floor lamp.

Magnifier

Check out drugstore glasses, visor magnifiers, magnifiers that attach to your lamp or work surface, and custom binocular magnifying telescopes. When choosing a magnifier, it is important to make sure it is comfortable. Find the balance between degree of magnification and depth of field—that means you need to be able to see both the tiny details in beadwork in your hands and keep the beads on your work surface in focus.

Tweezers with scoop

You will be surprised by how often you will pick up this lovely little tool with a scoop on one end and tweezers on the other. In addition to picking up beads, I use the scoop to sort or count beads, and the tweezers can be really helpful when tying knots.

Mini chainnose pliers

This may just be my favorite tool. These tiny 3-in. pliers are rounded on the outside and have a flat, smooth surface on the inside. I use them to gently pull a needle through a tight spot and break errant beads. They are also great for tying off short threads and pushing a bead to sit where it belongs.

Thread burner

A thread burner makes a clean burn and seals the ends of thread. The fine tip allows you to get in close when trimming the thread ends near the knots in your project. It is perfect for removing tiny, fuzzy frayed ends of thread or inevitable pesky bits of fuzz that escape from your foundation. Be careful, as it is easy to burn a hole in your foundation.

Foundation stretcher

Many textured bead embroidery techniques involve tightly compacted beads. For years, I was frustrated by curling, bending, and distortion of my beadwork. Stretching beading foundation on a wooden frame with a heavy-duty stapler or tacks can reduce most of the curling and distortion. Stretcher bar frames and unfinished wooden frames are available at craft stores. Avoid the ones designed to roll your fabric as you work. Those will crush your beads.

Markers

I use soft pastel pencils to sketch major details (borders, location of focal elements, clasp area, etc.) on my foundation. Charcoal gray works the best. For darker color foundations, choose a white pencil. Permanent markers are useful for drawing designs on your bead foundation or coloring backgrounds to match your beads.

Tape measure or ruler

My base tool kit contains both a tape measure and a 6-in. ruler. A tape measure (my Vera Bradley's is a gift from my son) is useful for laying out designs.

ADHESIVE

Terrifically Tacky Tape

Terrifically Tacky Tape is my adhesive of choice for attaching cabochons to bead foundation. It is easy to apply, refastenable, dries immediately, and has no odor. Just hold the cab in place while you bezel it. Your bezel should secure your cab to the foundation. This tape is not appropriate for gluing backing or other permanent objects which will not be bezeled.

Cut the tape to fit your cab (cut the corners for round or oval cabs), apply it to the back of your cab, and affix it to your foundation. You can begin beading immediately.

E6000 adhesive

To "permanently" adhere an element or apply the backing to my work, I prefer E6000. When using any adhesive, be sure to follow the manufacturer's instructions and only use adhesives in locations where there is plenty of fresh air moving through the room.

Poster board

Sometimes your bead embroidery needs a little support—the beads may be too heavy, your work may have curled due to excessive tension, or you may just want a very stiff piece. Cut a piece of poster board just smaller than your piece and glue it into your beadwork sandwich in the finishing phase.

Fundamental Techniques

Transferring designs to a foundation

You will need to transfer the templates and designs to your beading foundation. The simplest option, of course, is to draw it on with marker or pencil (use a white pencil for dark foundation).

Since drawing is not my forte, I have had the most success designing on the computer. I can then print my design right onto my foundation. Before

foundations were available in so many colors, I printed my background right on the fabric. Lacy's Stiff Stuff is the only product that is printer compatible. The CD included with this book has printable PDF templates for several collar and bracelet formats in a variety of sizes. Use these whenever directed.

For other foundations, or if your printer is less than cooperative with Lacy's, you can print your design on

iron-on transfer paper and then iron it on to your foundation. Lacy's now sells Self-Adhesive pattern sheets. You can photocopy or print your pattern on the pattern sheet and cut it out. Gently peel away the backing and apply it to the foundation. Embroider right through the pattern sheet. When you are finished, peel away any excess.

KNOTS

Quilter's knot

You need to anchor your thread every time you start a new section of beadwork. The quilter's knot technique puts a nice, tight knot at the very tip of your thread. Just pass your needle up through the foundation when starting a new thread, and the knot will catch and hold it in place.

1 Hold your threaded needle with one hand and the tail end of the thread with the other. We will now call these "needle hand" and "tail hand."

2 Position the needle horizontally. Place your needle on top of your thread, forming a T, so that just a teeny bit of thread extends above the needle. With the needle hand, pinch the tail of the thread down onto the shaft of the needle.

3 With the tail hand, begin winding the thread away from you onto the needle close to the pinched fingers on your needle. Keep the coils close together. Wind the thread three or four times. More wraps will create a bigger knot.

4 Without releasing your grip on the thread, carefully nudge the pinched

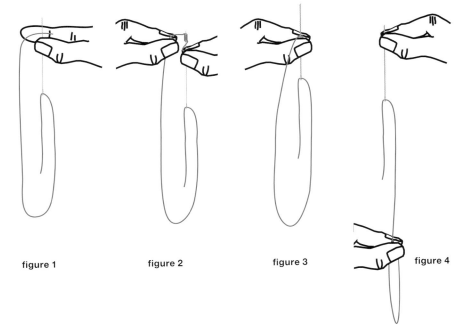

figure 1   figure 2   figure 3   figure 4

fingers holding your needle onto the coiled thread. Your fingers will stay gripped on these coils until the knot is completed.

5 With the future knot gripped tightly with the needle hand, release the tail end of the thread. Grab the tip of the needle with the tail hand. Pull the needle with your tail hand away from your needle hand while maintaining a good grip on the future knot in the pinched fingers

of your needle hand. Pull the needle until the entire length of thread has passed through the knot. A tight tug and you're done! A neat little knot will have formed at the end of your thread.

TIP: Start a new thread every time you finish an element. That way, it is safe and secure if you decide you are unhappy with whatever comes next. It is also protected if a thread breaks in another portion of your work.

Weaver's knot

I find the weaver's knot indispensible when my thread is too short either because I didn't end it soon enough or something caused it to break. Practice this at first using two different color thread or ribbons.

1 Hold your new thread vertically. Using your other hand, form a T by placing the existing thread horizontally on top of the new thread. The tip of each thread should extend approximately 2 in. beyond the intersection.

2 Hold the threads in one hand by pinching your thumb and finger where the two threads intersect. With the now free hand, grasp the lower end of the new thread and wrap it in a loop around the top of the T (which is actually the tip of your new thread) and over the tip of your existing thread.

3 Maintaining the loop, position the new thread so it also intersects at the T formed by the two threads. Slip the junction tightly under your thumb.

4 Take the tip of the existing thread and pass it through the loop. With your free hand, grasp the two segments of the new thread.

5 Relax your grip and grasp the two segments of the existing thread. Pull snugly with both hands until you hear a snap. You should now have a secure knot. Trim the tips of each thread at the knot and go back to work.

figure 1

figure 2

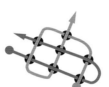

figure 3

figure 4

figure 5

TIP: If you knot Fireline with a weaver's knot, the knot might slide right out. For Fireline, tie a weaver's knot and then tie a square knot (right over left, left over right) on top of it.

Half-hitch knot

If you are working on the back of your foundation through existing stitches: Find a secure existing stitch where you want to knot. Slide your needle under that thread and form a small loop. Bring the needle through the loop and pull tight. Repeat several times.

    If you are working on the back of your foundation where stitches are not available, make a small stitch into your foundation but instead of pulling it tight, form a small loop. Bring the needle through the loop and pull tight. Repeat.

figure 1

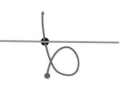

figure 2

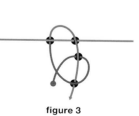

figure 3

If you are working between beads in your beadwork: Exit a bead and slide your needle under the existing thread between that bead and the next bead.

Form a small loop, bring the needle through the loop, and pull tight. Repeat.

BASIC STITCHES

Backstitch

The backstitch is the fundamental bead embroidery stitch. You will find many uses, including laying down horizontal lines of seed beads and starting the bezel of a cabochon.

1 Secure the thread with a quilter's knot, and pass through the foundation. Pick up two beads and slide them all the way back to the fabric **(figure 1)**. Position the needle next to the second bead, and pass straight down through the foundation **(figure 2)**.

2 Bring the needle up immediately adjacent to the first bead, and pass through both beads **(figure 3 and 4)**. Pick up two more beads and slide them against the first two beads **(figure 5)**.

3 Position the needle right next to the last bead you added, and pass straight down through the foundation **(figure 6)**. Bring your needle up between the first and second beads, and pass through the last three beads **(figure 7)**.

Continue as follows:
4 Pick up two beads. Position the needle right next to the last bead you added, and pass straight down through the foundation **(figure 8)**.

5 Count back three beads, including the two beads you are now adding, and pass through the second bead of the previous pair and the two beads you just added **(figures 9 and 10)**. You are ready to add the next two beads. You will get a sense of the bead spacing—trust your intuition.

TIP: Passing your thread through a row of beads a second (or third) time reinforces the element and encourages the beads to lay straight, smooth, and in the right position. The extra thread fill up the bead holes, and by altering where you pass your needle back through the foundation, you can force difficult beads to stay put.

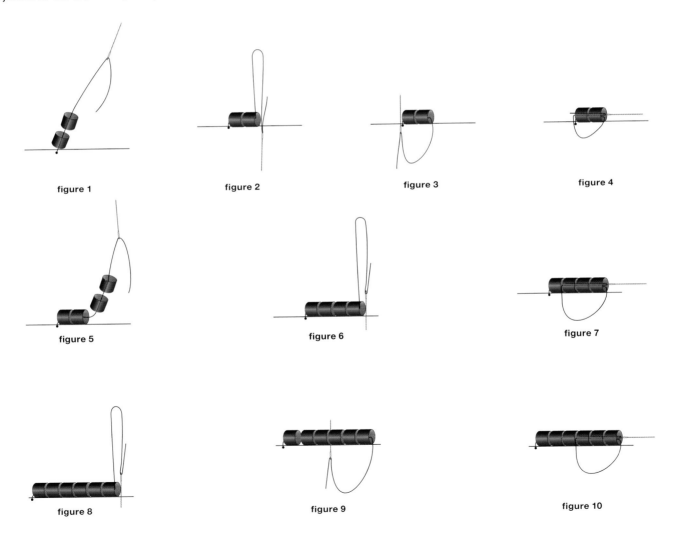

figure 1

figure 2

figure 3

figure 4

figure 5

figure 6

figure 7

figure 8

figure 9

figure 10

TIP: Needle angle is critical. When passing your needle through the foundation, make sure it is straight (perpendicular to the foundation). The angle of your needle significantly affects how your beads lie. If your needle passes through the foundation at an angle the beads may end up too far apart (thread shows) or too tight against each other (which causes your row to pucker). Keeping your needle straight also helps to prevent splitting threads on the back and having your beads roll under your cabochon when stitching a bezel.

Stop stitch

Any bead (from a seed bead to a pearl or a lampworked gem) can become a design element when applied using the stop stitch. A stop bead is a bead or beads used to hold your design bead in place. Here are a few varieties of the stop stitch:

Simple stop bead

The simple stop bead is the most common. Use a smaller bead to secure your decorative bead. Pass up through the foundation in the exact spot you wish your bead to sit. Pick up the decorative bead and a stopper bead. Bypass the stop bead, and pass down through the design element bead and foundation. Repeat if the bead is heavy or sharp **(figures 1 and 2)**.

Picot stop stitch

Your stopper bead can become a design element, such as the picot. Pass up through the foundation in

the exact spot you wish your bead to sit. Pick up your bead and three stop beads. Bypass the three stop beads, and pass down through the design element bead and your foundation. The three stopper beads form a little point. Repeat if the bead is heavy or sharp **(figures 3 and 4)**.

Stack stitch

You can add another bead between the design element and the stopper bead to create more interest. Pick up a design element bead, a secondary decorative bead, and a stopper bead. Bypass the stopper bead and pass down through the secondary decorative bead, the design element bead, and the foundation **(figures 5 and 6)**. If the bead is heavy or sharp, you may want to repeat. Use your imagination to layer beads in a variety of combinations.

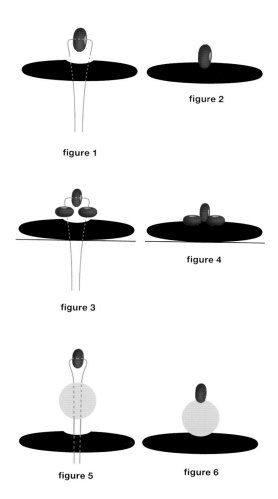

figure 1

figure 2

figure 3

figure 4

figure 5

figure 6

Even-count tubular peyote stitch

For bead embroidery, always begin peyote stitch on a backstitch foundation.

Begin with round three

1 Once you have completed your backstitch row, pass through the first two beads you stitched to connect the ring. Pick up a bead, skip the next bead in the backstitch row, and pass through the following bead **(figure 1)**. This is the first bead in round three. The new bead should stack on top of the bead you passed over. Use your fingers to help it if it is not sitting properly **(figure 2)**.

2 Pick up a bead, skip a bead, and pass through the next bead **(figure 3)**. Repeat until you return to where you started. At this point, there doesn't seem to be a place to add the next bead. That's because it is time for your step up—you are moving up to start the next round. Without picking up a bead, pass through the first bead you added in round three **(figure 4)**.

3 At this point, there should now be "up" beads and "down" beads. The up-beads are like little teeth sticking up above

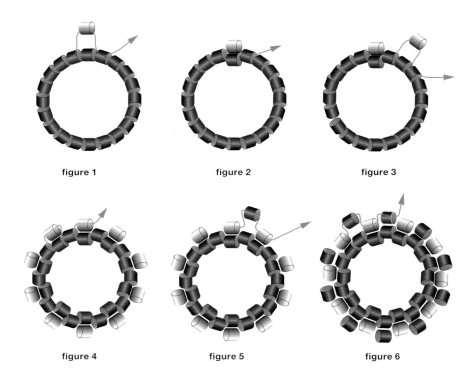

figure 1　　　figure 2　　　figure 3

figure 4　　　figure 5　　　figure 6

the down beads. You will essentially be filling in the spaces between the up or protruding beads in the previous round. Pick up a bead and pass through the first protruding bead in round three **(figure 5)**. You have now started round four. Pick up a bead, and pass through the next up-bead. Repeat until you return to where you started.

4 After you add the last bead, pass through the first bead you added in round four **without** picking up a bead **(figure 6)**. This is your "step-up." You are now ready to start round five.

5 Repeat until you have completed the desired number of rounds.

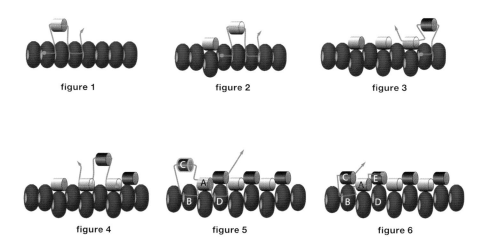

figure 1　　　figure 2　　　figure 3

figure 4　　　figure 5　　　figure 6

Odd-count flat peyote stitch (from backstitch or a bezel)

For bead embroidery, odd-count flat peyote stitch is worked off a backstitch foundation or existing peyote stitch, such as a bezel. Be sure to begin with an odd number of beads in the backstitch row.

Begin with round three

1 With your thread exiting the first bead in the backstitch row, pick up a bead, skip the next bead in the backstitch row, and pass through the following bead **(figure 1)**. This is the first bead in row three. The new bead should stack on top of the bead you passed over.

2 Pick up a bead, skip a bead, and pass through the next bead **(figure 2)**. Pull this bead snug. Repeat until your row is the desired length. For all future rows fill in the spaces between the "up" or protruding beads in the previous row.

3 The next row will be worked in the opposite direction. Pick up a bead, turn around, and pass through the bead you just added (the last bead on the previous row) **(figure 3)**. Pick up a bead and pass through the next up-bead **(figure 4)**.

4 Continue in this manner until you reach the end of the row. You need to add another bead in this row, with an odd-count flat peyote turn. There are several options, but I like the figure-eight turn. When you are working from a backstitch row, for the very first turn only you need to reposition your needle by passing though beads in the backstitch row. Your thread is exiting bead A. Pass down through bead B in the backstitch row. Pick up a bead C. Working in the opposite direction, sew through beads A and D **(figure 5)**.

5 Turn around and sew through beads E and A, pulling the thread snug so it hides between the beads. Pass through bead B in the backstitch row. Turn around and pass through bead C **(figure 6)**, and proceed as usual on the subsequent row. As you work, you will be alternating between odd and even turns. When you reach the next odd-count turn, you will follow the same series of steps, this time working off the previous peyote row.

Odd-count flat peyote stitch (from a peyote base)

When you work flat odd-count peyote stitch off an existing peyote stitch base, you use the existing up-beads. To start, fill in the spaces between the up-beads or protruding beads in the base.

1 Sew through the beadwork so your thread is exiting the bead where you want your flat peyote to start. Pick up a bead, skip the bead adjacent to where your thread is exiting, and pass through the next up-bead. Pull this bead snug. Repeat until your row is the desired length **(figures 1–5)**.

2 Follow the directions above for making the second odd-count turn **(figure 6)**.

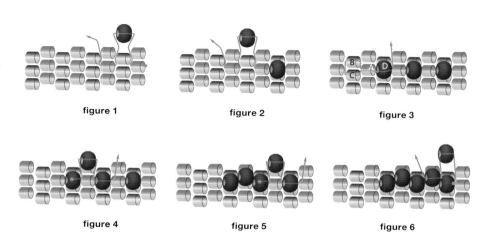

figure 1   figure 2   figure 3

figure 4   figure 5   figure 6

WORKING WITH CABOCHONS

Bezeling a cabochon

The classic description of a cabochon (or cab) is a domed stone with a flat bottom that does not have a hole drilled into it— but I have used everything from a slice of a vintage billiard ball to a glass vase filler as a cab. For the purposes of textured bead embroidery, a cab can be any size, shape, color, or material. While a flat bottom makes things easier, there are ways to make most shapes work. Ideally, the cab should have a beveled edge and a level, even finish. Avoid cabs with sharp edges. They can cut your thread and cause bends in your bezel.

The purpose of a bezel is to encase the cab and secure it to the foundation. The bezel, not the adhesive, is what keeps the cab there. A cab is bezeled to the foundation using a progression of bead sizes—from large to small.

TIP: Backstitch is used to start the peyote bezel of a cabochon. The bezel will only work if you use even-count tubular peyote stitch. If you only add two beads at a time, you will always have an even number of beads. You'll also have more control. I have found that I had a neater and smoother line when I used two beads. I recommend that you always use two beads for a bezel application. For all other uses, find your number.

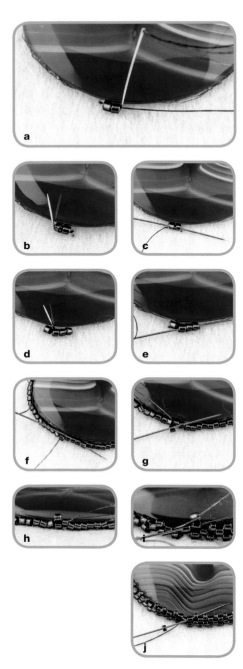

a

b

c

d

e

f

g

h

i

j

TIP: If you use a transparent or translucent cabochon, a dark foundation can change the color and cloud the beauty of the stone. Cut out a piece of white foundation a bit larger than the cab and adhere it to your foundation with Terrifically Tacky Tape. Tape your cab on top of the white patch, and bezel as usual.

A bezel can start with any size bead. It should be chosen in proportion to the size of your cab. The most common approach is to start with 11º cylinders and finish with a 15º seed bead. If you use 15º Charlottes for the top row, you will probably have to switch to a #13 beading needle. If the cab is slightly uneven, start with larger beads at the base to cover the "sins." The number of rounds needed will be determined by the height of your cab, the size of your beads, and the tension of your work.

1 Use adhesive (E6000 or Terrifically Tacky Tape) to adhere the cab to the beading foundation. Don't let the glue or tape extend to the edge of the stone.

2 Thread a beading needle with a single-strand of thread in a comfortable length, and tie a small **weaver's knot (p. 13)** at the end. Pass the needle up through the foundation very close to the edge of the cab to anchor the thread.

3 Backstitch (p. 14) a "frame" around your cab: Pick up two beads and slide them down to the cab as close as possible to the point where the thread exits the foundation. Pass the needle down through the foundation at the edge of the second bead **(photo a)**.

Pass the needle back up through the foundation before the first bead, staying close to the edge of the cab **(photo b)**. Pass the needle through both beads **(photo c)**.

4 Pick up two more beads, and push them down to the cab as close as possible to the existing beads. Pass the needle down through the foundation at the edge of the second bead. Count back three beads, including the two beads you are now adding. Pass the needle back up through the foundation before the third bead, staying close to the edge of the cab **(photo d)**. Pass the needle through the three beads **(photo e)**. You are now in position to add two more beads. Because the cab will be bezeled using tubular even-count peyote, you must add two beads at a time to ensure that there is an even number of beads.

5 Continue to add beads in this manner, staying close to the edge of the cab. If you stitch too close, the beads have a tendency to roll under the cab. If that happens, your bezel will be too small to encase the cab. Keep your beads stitched close together as you proceed around the cab, but do not squeeze them into each other. It is okay if there are slight gaps between beads, but avoid large gaps, which may cause holes in the bezel. (If there is not enough room for two beads in the space for the last stitch, leave the small gap.)

6 When you have surrounded the cab, pass the needle through the very first bead you stitched to connect the beads **(photo f)**. This ring of beads will become rounds one and two of your peyote bezel. Don't worry if your backstitching is irregular or a little sloppy. The beads will usually fall into place with the next peyote round. If all else fails, embellish.

7 Using even-count tubular peyote stitch **(p. 16)**, work round three of the bezel. Pick up a bead, skip the next bead, and pass the needle through the next bead. Pull snugly so that the bead you just added stands up on top of the bead beneath it **(photos g and h)**. Add beads in this manner until you have gone around the entire cab. Because you are working in tubular even-count peyote stitch, you have to step up through the first bead you added in round three to get into position for the next round **(photo i)**.

8 Continue stitching peyote rounds until the level of the beadwork reaches the edge of the dome of the cab. At this point, switch to a smaller bead and continue stitching peyote rounds **(photo j)**. Pull snug so your beadwork tightens up over the dome of the cab. It may need just two rounds of the smaller beads, or as many as three or four. Make sure your beadwork encases the cab.

9 When you are finished, sew down through the beadwork, making certain the thread is hidden, and pass down through the foundation. Secure and trim the thread on the back of your work.

Bezeling a cabochon with angles

When working with a square or triangle-shaped cabochon, the bezel may gap in the corners. Try skipping a stitch in the corners after the third round. When you reach the corner, pass through the next up-bead without picking up a bead—just bring the needle straight from one bead to another. Don't worry if the thread shows. When you reach that spot in the next round, add a single bead in the large space left in the previous pass. Pull the thread to snug up the space.

If another round is required, work peyote stitch as normal. Not all shapes can be bezeled using traditional methods, especially anything with an inside curve. When you begin to tighten your bezel around a cabochon with an inside curve, the bezel wall on the inside curve will tighten up as if that side was straight, leaving a gap between the bezel and the cab.

Bezel finishes

Now that you know how to construct the bezel, you can start thinking how to best frame the cabochon.

Pick a color scheme **(photo a)**. Try monochromatic colors: You can create a very subtle bezel using two or three sizes of beads in the same color, which can be very useful when you plan to embellish the bezel. You can also use complementary colors: Pick two or more colors from your palette. I usually start with a more neutral color and finish off with a highlight color that really showcases the cab.

Try "oops" edging **(photo b)**: Sometimes the 15° seed bead or Charlotte does not fill the gap between the larger beads in the previous row. Consider adding two beads in the final row of the bezel. It will create a gently rolling edge and cover the gaps in the bezel.

Choose decorative edging **(photo c)**: Think outside the box. Finish off a large cab with drops instead of seed beads, for example.

Embellishing a bezel: stitch in the ditch

"Stitch in the ditch" is an embellishment technique built on a foundation created using one of the basic beadweaving stitches. It involves weaving through the rows again, picking up-beads as you go, and stitching between and sometimes on top of the beads in the base. It is most frequently done on top of an existing layer of peyote.

In bead embroidery, the bezel around a cabochon is created in peyote stitch. You also use peyote stitch for bails or connector strips. With your thread exiting the desired bead, pick up a bead, and sew through the next bead in the same row **(figures 1 and 2)**. Repeat across the row or as directed **(figure 3)**.

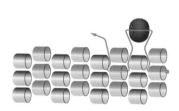

figure 1

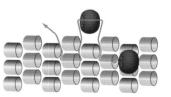

figure 2

figure 3

WORKING WITH BAILS

Odd-count peyote bail and zipping up

Using odd-count peyote allows you to have a balanced bail with a distinct center.

1 Decide how many beads wide you want the bail (obviously, it is an odd number). Subtract one (the center bead) and divide the remaining number by two. This is how many beads from the center bead your bail will extend. The first step is essentially a **stitch in the ditch (p. 19)**, working off the peyote stitch bezel. Identify where you want the center of your bail to sit. It must be an up-bead.

2 Using the number calculated in step one, count that many beads to one side of the center bead. That is the outside bead. It also must be an up-bead. Pass through the beadwork so the thread is exiting the outside bead of the bezel, with the needle pointing toward the center bead.

3 Work in **flat odd-count peyote (figure 1, p. 17)** until your strip is twice the desired length of your bail. There must be an even number of rows in order to zip up the bail. When you are finished, the thread will exit the top left bead.

4 Before attaching the bail to the back of the cab, lock in the last bead on the final row by weaving through an adjacent bead and back through the final bead **(figure 2)**.

5 Fold the top of the bail toward the back of the cab. Follow the thread path to "zip" the edge of the bail to the top of the bezel **(figure 3)**. You will have to leave the thread loose in order to be able to get through the beads, but you need to gently pull tight as you go so the bail is completely interlocked into the bezel.

6 Reinforce the connection by following the thread path in the opposite direction **(figure 4)**. Secure the thread.

TIP: The easiest way to count peyote rows is to pick a bottom corner and identify the first two vertical columns. Starting with the lowest bead, count the beads by zigzagging back and forth between the two columns. Use a beading needle as a pointer to help you keep your place while counting.

figure 1

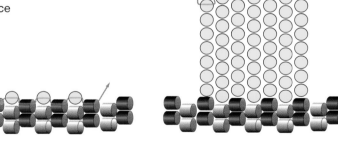

figure 2

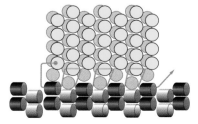

figure 3

figure 4

Whipstitch edging

1 With a thread exiting a bead along the outer edge of the bail (in the diagram, that would be the first bead on row two), pick up a seed bead and pass under the thread connecting peyote rows two and four **(figure 1)**.

2 Pull gently, and the bead will sit on the edge of the bail between the two beads.

3 Pick up a seed bead, and pass under the thread connecting the next two peyote rows (four and six) **(figure 2)**.

4 Repeat until you have embellished along the entire length.

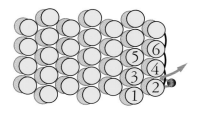

figure 1

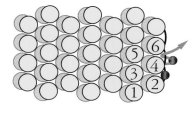

figure 2

SPECIAL TECHNIQUES

Clustering

A cluster is simply a group of beads stitched tightly together. You can cluster almost any type of bead for more dimension, texture, and interest. It can take any shape you choose. For added excitement, incorporate different beads in the cluster. See the **Bead Directory (p. 34)** for suggestions on how to cluster specific beads.

1 Always work from the center of the cluster toward the edges. Pass through the foundation where you want your bead to sit, pick up your bead (or your bead and a stop bead) and pass back into the foundation at almost the same point. Some beads work best alone. Some need a stop bead.

2 Pass up through the foundation in the exact spot you wish the next bead to sit. It should be positioned right against the previous bead. Pick up a bead and pass back into the foundation at almost the same point. Pull tightly so that the beads cluster together. Repeat, adding beads in every direction, until you are satisfied with the size of the cluster.

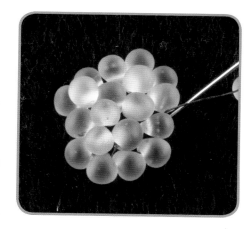

TIP: When beads simply refuse to cooperate and all else fails, I "utz." Utz is a Yiddish word meaning to goad, annoy, or bother— to provoke or stimulate some reaction. Stop and think about where you want the bead to go, and determine what it would take to make it happen. That dagger still won't stand up after you built that support row? Try another row of beads. Place a big bead on top of a bead that won't lie down. Cover an obstinate gap with a decorative bead. Remember, necessity is the mother of invention!

Python technique

One of the distinctive characteristics of textured bead embroidery is using of beads in an unfamiliar orientation to create interesting patterns. The python technique, which uses seed bead triangles, or hex beads, is a wonderful example.

The python is simply clusters of 8° or 11° hex or triangle beads embroidered vertically using **stop stitch (p. 15)**. First, draw the path you want your python to follow on the foundation. Starting on one end, embroider the beads one at a time using stop stitch. Position these beads carefully because the first row defines the path of all future rows.

• 8° seed beads work up quickly and create a bolder element. For a more refined, almost fabric looking effect, use 11°s.

• The stop bead should be the smallest possible that won't slip through the hole in the bead. For an 8° triangle or hex, I recommend 15°s. 15° Charlottes are also effective with 11°s.

• For a more striking effect, use a stop bead in a contrasting color. For a subtle look, match the stop bead to the triangle or hex. I have also used clear crystal Charlottes that do not affect the color of the base bead.

• For the python technique, beads with sharp, crisp corners yield the best results. The Miyuki Delica "cut bead" is also hexagonally shaped and effective for the Python.

• **Cull your beads** (separate out the flawed beads). Look for beads that are irregularly shaped, have sharp edges, are thinner or fatter than the others, or are discolored; discard them.

Using triangles in python technique

The trick to applying triangles is to alternate the direction of the triangles. Place the first triangle so that its point is on the line. Sew the second up against the first with a flat face on the line. The third reverts to the point on the line and the fourth is applied with a flat face on the line **(photo a)**. Continue this pattern for the rest of the line. When bringing your thread up from the back, position it where you want the center of the triangle to be. When passing back through the foundation to secure it, pull it close to the adjacent row of beads. Occasionally you may have to help an uncooperative triangle by gently correcting its position with a tweezers, pliers or your fingers. Do not be concerned if the first row seems a bit awkward; the beads will line up as you sew future rows. Change direction and follow the same pattern with the second row snugly alongside the first. Repeat until you have filled the allotted space **(photo b)**. As you follow a curve, the triangles contour very well if you pull your thread firmly. Do not pull against the edge of the bead, or it will cut your thread.

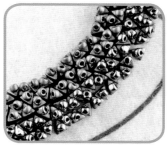

Using hex beads in python technique

Hex beads lock neatly into place because there are twice as many surfaces. Position the first hex bead so that one face is on the line. The next bead will sit tightly against the first. Continue this pattern for the rest of the line. When you finish the first row, change directions and begin filling the spaces between the beads with the next row. They should lock neatly in place. Carefully aligning each row as you sew, repeat this process until you have filled the allotted space **(photo c)**. I was surprised to learn that hex beads are not as forgiving when you are following a curve. At close magnification, you will see little spaces between the beads, but they are not noticeable in the finished effect.

Layering and overlapping

I love to stack beads on top of each other, whether it is a simple **stack stitch (p. 15)** or an elaborate grouping of beads in multiple levels. Layering is one of the best ways to create texture, dimension, and drama.

One of my favorite techniques is to **backstitch (p. 14)** a geometrically oriented bed of beads and position stack stitches of larger distinctive beads on top.

Layering also works great on a bed of tightly clustered tiny drop beads or rows of backstitched round seed beads. Let your highlight beads overlap multiple elements for a more unified connection between neighboring sections. Embellish the cabs to give your work more depth and interest.

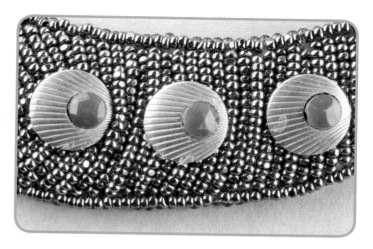

Support rows

Some beads need "help" to sit properly. This is where "support beads" come in to play. Use backstitch rows, stop stitch beads, or even clusters to "encourage" uncooperative beads to sit the way you want. I often hide support beads under the decorative beads to make them stand up or sit at the angle I want. I have also created a decorative element in front of wayward beads to force them to stay down or lie at a different angle.

Backstitch (p. 14) a row of small beads to support the bead **(photos a and b)**. Stitch the bead very close to the backstitch row if you want them more erect. Leave a little space between the backstitch row and the beads if you want them to slant. The beads will essentially be "leaning" on the backstitch row. The size of your backstitched beads will also influence the slope of your beads. The larger the bead, the greater the angle.

Stitch a tight cluster of beads for a decorative way to control the errant beads. You can convince your beads to stay in the position you want, depending on where you place the cluster. Place it on top of the base of the beads to convince them to lean. Position it under or behind your bead to support it. Consider positioning the cluster so that it overlaps any uncooperative beads.

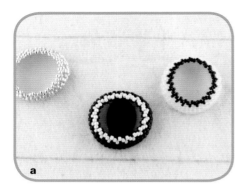

Order of application

The order in which you apply your beads makes a big difference. If you decide to elaborately embellish a cabochon, it is going to be really frustrating later if you want to cover the foundation under the embellishment. Here is how I typically approach a piece:

1 Place and bezel cabochon(s) **(photo a)**.

2 Stitch an element that dictates the overall flow of the piece—a line that winds through the design often dictated by the patterns and colors of the cab.

3 Frame the cab(s) with base beads that will probably be obscured by embellishments later **(photo b)**.

4 Embellish the cab(s) **(photo c)**.

5 Start filling in between the elements wherever my needle takes me.

While the clasp is always added last, it is important to decide where you will place it early in the process, because that decision will dramatically affect the adjacent portion of the beadwork.

TIP: With bead embroidery, you can make corrections or changes, as long as you knot off and start a new thread every time you complete an element. If you change your mind, you can tear it out and start the section over; bead over it, which can result in some great effects; or cut it up for use in a future project.

FINISHING

Backing

When you've completed your design, knot the thread on the back and trim. Carefully cut around your design as close as possible without cutting any threads **(photo a)**. Apply glue to the back of your beadwork **(photo b)** and place the glued side down on your backing. After the glue has dried, carefully cut the beadwork/backing sandwich to the desired shape, making sure you do not cut any threads **(photo c)**. Edge your work with one of the edging stitches shown. **Brick stitch edging (p. 26)** is best when you plan to add fringe to your work. **Blanket stitch edging (p. 26)** is best when you want to hide the edge of your beadwork/backing sandwich.

Brass cuffs or collars

Brass cuffs and collars are available in a variety of widths and sizes. They slip on and off easily, but they are a little more difficult to finish than some of the other options.

Create a design that is ⅛ in. larger than the brass blank in every direction. Remember to allow for shrinkage. Cut a piece of backing that is ½ in. wider than your blank in every direction. Glue the backing to the underside of the brass blank, using a stick to spread the glue, and work from the middle out, making sure there are no air bubbles. Do not trim. Let dry.

When you've completed your design, secure your thread on the back. Hold your work up to the blank to be certain it extends beyond the cuff ⅛ in. on all sides. Carefully cut around your design as close as possible without cutting any threads. Your beadwork should be ⅛ in. larger than the blank in every direction.

Apply glue to the back of the beadwork. Because the glue will spread when the beadwork is pressed to the blank and you still have to pass your needle through the edges, leave a small margin without glue around the edge. Place the glued side on the brass blank, making sure it is positioned correctly on the cuff. After the glue has dried for at least 20 minutes, trim the backing to match the beadwork. It should still extend ⅛ in. all the way around the cuff.

You now have a beadwork/blank/backing sandwich. Edge the work with one of the **edging stitches (p. 26)**.

TIP: Many recipes end with the phrase, "adjust the seasoning." Bead embroidery is no different. You may find little bare or sparse spots once you have finished edging your work. Pull out your needle and fill them in, but remember that you can only work on the surface once you have finished the back. Pass through the other beads to secure your thread.

Edging

Use enough thread to go around the entire project without having to change it. I strongly recommend that you match your thread to the backing color.

Blanket stitch edging

Use blanket stitch bead edging when you have no plan to add fringe to the finished edges of your bead embroidery. It gives a more finished edge to the work.

1 Tie a knot at the end of the thread and trim it closely. Bury it between the foundation and the backing. Bring the thread out through the edge of the foundation **(figure 1)**.

2 Pick up a bead, and pass up through both layers. Pass back through your bead in the direction you are working. Your bead will sit on the edge of the two layers at a slight angle **(figure 2)**.

4 Pick up a new bead and pass up through both layers **(figure 3)**.

5 Pass back through your bead in the direction you are working **(figure 4)**.

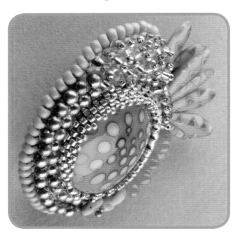

Your bead will sit on the edge of the two layers at a slight angle **(figure 5)**.

6 Repeat steps 2–5 until you have edged the whole piece. Pass through the first bead to connect the last bead. Secure the thread by passing through a few beads and tying a hidden **half-hitch knot (p. 13)**. Repeat twice; trim the thread.

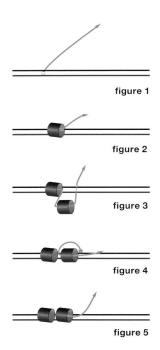

figure 1

figure 2

figure 3

figure 4

figure 5

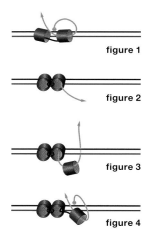

figure 1

figure 2

figure 3

figure 4

Brick stitch edging

Use brick stitch bead edging when you plan to add fringe to the finished edges of your bead embroidery.

1 Hide the knot under the beadwork as in **blanket stitch edging (figure 1)**.

2 With the needle exiting the top edge of the beadwork, pick up two beads and sew up through both layers. Pass your needle up through the second seed bead, pulling snug **(figure 2)**. The beads will stand out from the edge of the piece **(figure 3)**.

3 Pick up one bead, and pass the needle through the both layers **(figure 4)**. Bring the needle back up through the bead just added.

4 Continue around in this manner. The idea is to connect the two layers

together. When you've edged the whole way around and the last bead meets the first bead you sewed, go down through the first bead to attach the two.

5 Pass the needle through some beads, tying several small knots in the beadwork and "hiding" them in the beads. Trim the thread as close to the beadwork as you can, taking care not to cut your work.

Fringe

Some of the most dramatic bead embroidered collars and earrings I have seen have been embellished by fabulous, abundant fringe. Dramatic fringe is often just too much when added to my textured, dimensional style of bead embroidery, but there are some cases where fringe can be used effectively to add drama and interest.

If you plan to add fringe, use **brick stitch edging (p. 26)** to finish your work. Each strand of fringe will be suspended from a brick-stitched bead. Almost any bead or combination of beads can be used in fringe. The length can be uniform, graduated, contoured, or varied. Before we get into the mechanics, here are a few tips to assist you when choosing your beads:

• Use bigger/heavier beads at the bottom to help weight the fringe both physically and visually. Choice of beads can affect the drape of the fringe. For example, round seed beads seem to drape better than cylinder beads (for the same reasons, I prefer round seed beads for backstitch lines).

• Remember that the use of beads in an unfamiliar orientation is one of the distinctive characteristics of textured bead embroidery. Think outside the lines!

• Consider wearability when designing fringe. How will the fringe lay when a real person wears the necklace? You can spread the fringe out for dramatic effect

on a flat surface, but when worn, gravity brings that fringe straight down. While still pretty, it is not as effective.

• Tie a half-hitch knot every few fringes. This minimizes the damage if your fringe should catch or break.

• Your fringe should follow the lines of your necklace or earring.

• Consider placing fringe in unexpected places. Who says it has to be at the bottom of the necklace?

• Use a variety of fringe techniques within the same piece.

Starting fringe

When starting any fringe, knot a comfortable length of thread and secure it by burying it inside the foundation/backing sandwich or between rows of beads so no thread shows. Stitch through the very edge of the foundation (under the edge bead, top layer only) at a right angle with the edging and through the appropriate brick stitch bead. With this method, there is no visible thread on the back of your piece, and passing both through the fabric and the edge bead strengthens and reinforces the fringe (especially if it is heavy fringe).

TIP: Pay close attention to your tension when adding fringe. You want it tight enough that no thread is visible, but relaxed enough to drape nicely. If the tension is too loose, the fringe is limp, thread shows, and it hangs awkwardly. If you pull too tight, your fringe will be stiff and the beads may fold against each other.

Straight fringe

1 Thread the beads for the first fringe, ending with a drop, dangle, Charlotte, or 15° seed bead. Make sure that the length is proportional to your beadwork.

2 Skip the final bead in the fringe, and sew through the rest of the beads again (in the opposite direction), into the edge bead, and through the very edge of the foundation (under the edge bead, upper layer only). I find the easiest way to tighten the fringe is to slide the fringe beads into position, hold onto the end bead, and gently pull straight up through the edge bead.

3 Once you are satisfied with the drape of the first fringe, bring the thread through the next edge bead (remember that you have already reinforced your thread through the foundation when you came up from the previous fringe) **(figures 1 and 2)**. Continue until you have completed the fringe. Secure the thread with half-hitch knots hidden under beads, and trim.

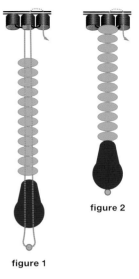

figure 2

figure 1

Bail-ended fringe

1 If your final element is a drop or other dangle where the placement of the hole makes it impossible to hang it without exposed thread, pick up in this order: your base length of fringe, enough seed beads to cover any possible exposed thread (it will take trial and error), your drop or dangle, and the same number of seed beads added previously.

2 Pass back through your base length of fringe, working in the opposite direction. The small seed beads will form a bail around your drop or dangle **(figures 1 and 2)**.

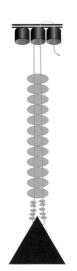

figure 2

figure 1

CLASPS AND CLOSURES

For me, one of the most challenging parts of bead embroidery is finding clasps and closures that are easy for the wearer to use, strong enough to support the piece, and aesthetically appealing. Here are just a few ideas.

Hook-and-eye clasp

There are an amazing variety and sizes of hook-and-eye options in a sewing store's notions department. Choose one that is large enough and strong enough to hold the weight of your beadwork. To prevent twisting when wearing a bracelet, consider using two sets (three sets for a wider bracelet) or one that has several connections. Hooks and eyes are added when you are completely finished assembling and edging your piece.

1 Attach the eyes first. Position the first eye so that it protrudes ⅛ in. from the edging on the end of your piece and one of the loops touches the side edge beads. Identify the edge bead closest to this loop.

2 Start a thread, but do not knot. Bring the thread through a bead in the side edging about 2 in. from the bead you identified in the previous step. Leave a 6-in. tail protruding from the bead you entered. This will be trimmed off later. Make a **half-hitch knot (p. 13)**. Working toward where you want the eye, pass through three more beads. Tie another half-hitch knot. Repeat **(figure 1)**.

3 Pass through the side edge beads until you exit the bead closest to the loop. Pass through the loop and back through the side edge bead. Repeat several times until that loop is secure **(figure 2)**. Slide the needle between the suede and beading foundation and under the eye until it reaches the other loop on the opposite side of the eye **(figure 3)**. Pass through the loop and into the suede. Repeat several times until that loop is secure. Slide the needle between the suede and beading foundation until it reaches the edging **(figure 4)**.

4 Position the second eye so it protrudes ⅛ in. from the end edging and one of the loops touches the side edge beads. Identify the edge bead closest to the loop. Pass through the edge beads until you reach the bead closest to the loop. Work as before to secure this eye to the work. For a wider bracelet, add a third eye centered between the other two eyes **(figure 5)**.

5 Repeat steps 1–4 on the other side of the bracelet using the hooks. Make sure that each of the hooks matches up to the eye on the other side **(figure 6)**. Use pliers to adjust the opening of the hook to make it easier to fasten.

figure 1

figure 2

figure 3

figure 4

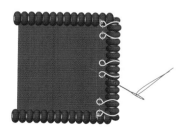

figure 5

figure 6

Loop-and-button closure

One of the simplest closures is a button on one side and a beaded loop to hold it in place on the other. For added security and stability, consider two or more parallel button-and-loop sets. If possible, the loop and button should be attached before the backing is added.

Always do the button first. It is much easier to adjust the size of the loop to accommodate the size of the button. When choosing the position of your button, take into consideration that the two ends should overlap slightly when fastened.

There are two basic types of buttons distinguished by how the button is attached to the fabric: Shank buttons have a small ring or a bar with a hole protruding from the back of the button, and sew-through buttons have holes in the face.

I like to put a flat rondelle at the base of both the button and the loop. It gives the closure a more polished look, and it elevates a sew-through button, making it easier for the loop to catch underneath it.

Shanked button

1 Using double thread, bring your needle up through the foundation where you want your button to sit. Pick up a flat rondelle and enough small beads to form a loop inside the shank **(figure 1)**. Sew through the shank, back through the rondelle, and into the foundation.

2 Gently pull tight so that the shank sits flush against the bracelet and the small beads form a loop that passes inside the shank. To secure the button, repeat as many times as you can get your needle through the beads, knotting occasionally. Trim. Repeat for another button **(figure 2)**.

Sew-through button

1 Using double thread, bring your needle up through the foundation. Pick up a flat rondelle, and pass through the first hole in your button. The configuration of your button determines what you do next: I like to pick up a few small beads before passing through the opposite hole in the button **(figure 3 and 4)**.

2 Sew back through the rondelle and into the foundation. Gently pull tight so that the button sits flush against the rondelle and the work. To secure the

button, repeat several times, knotting occasionally. Trim.

Loop

There are also two choices for the loop end of your closure. Your loop can emanate from one (ring-shaped) or two (u-shaped) spots. The figures show a u-shaped loop **(figure 5)**.

1 On the end of the piece, opposite the button, pass up through the foundation where you want the loop to be. Thread a disk or rondelle and enough beads to create a loop that will fit the button.

2 Keeping the thread tension tight, test the loop size with your button. Add or remove beads as necessary.

3 Pass back down through the foundation at the appropriate spot. Pull so the loop and rondelle sit firmly against the surface of your beadwork and the loop is taut but not stretched too tightly (the beads should not bend against each other). Test the fit **(figure 6)**. Pass through the loop as many times as your beads will allow, knotting occasionally. Knot. Once the loop is secured, trim the thread.

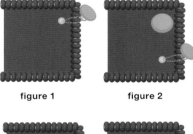

figure 1   figure 2

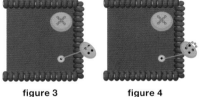

figure 3   figure 4

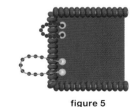

figure 5

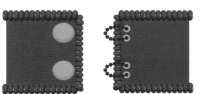

figure 6

Attaching a bar clasp

Edge your finished project with brick stitch or blanket stitch edging. Working off this edging, stitch a peyote-stitch strap which will be used to attach your clasp to the piece.

Working off blanket stitch edging

1 Position your thread so that it is exiting the bead where you want your band to start. Pick up a bead, skip the adjacent bead, and pass through the next bead. The new bead should stack on top of the bead you skipped. Use your fingers to help it if it is not sitting properly.

2 Pick up a bead, skip a bead, and pass through the next bead. Repeat until your band is the correct width to fit into the clasp structure.

3 Follow the instructions for **flat odd-count peyote stitch (p. 17)** until you have completed the number of rows necessary to comfortably pass through the clasp and return to the edging. There must be an even number of rows in order to zip up your band.

4 Lock in the last bead on the final row by weaving through an adjacent bead and back through the final bead **(figure 1)**. This will prevent your bead-work from loosening up when you attach the band. Pass the band through the bar of the clasp.

5 Fold the band holding the clasp until it meets the edging. Follow the thread path to zip the edge of the band to the bracelet **(figure 2)**. Leave the thread loose in order to be able to get through the beads, but gently pull tight as you go so the band is completely interlocked into the bezel.

6 Reinforce the connection by following the thread path in the opposite direction. Secure the thread. Repeat with the other side of the clasp.

figure 1

figure 2

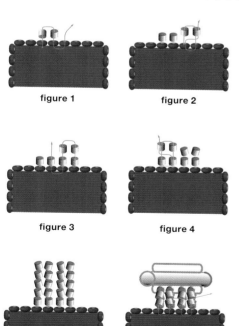

figure 1

figure 2

figure 3

figure 4

figure 5

figure 6

Working off brick stitch edging

1 If you have edged in brick stitch, create a flat herringbone stitch band, using the edge beads as a base.

2 Position your thread so that it is exiting the bead where you want your band to start. Pick up two beads, and pass down through the adjacent edge bead and up through the following edge bead **(figure 1)**.

3 Pick up two beads, and pass down through the next bead and up through the following bead. Repeat until your band is the correct width to fit into the clasp structure.

4 To make the turn: Pass back up through the bead your thread was exiting at the beginning of this stitch and then through the last bead added **(figure 2)**.

5 Work as in steps 2–4 in the opposite direction **(figures 3 and 4)**. Continue in this manner until you have completed the number of rows necessary to pass comfortably through the clasp and return to the edging **(figure 5)**. Keeping in mind that bar clasps often have a distinct front and back, pass the band through the bar of the clasp.

6 Next, attach the band to the brick stitched edging: Fold the band until it meets the edging. Work your thread up and down through edge beads until the band is secure **(figure 6)**.

7 Reinforce the connection by following the thread path in the opposite direction. Secure the thread. Repeat with the other side of the clasp.

Bead sandwich clasp

You can make a wonderful clasp by layering multiple sizes of beads into a large bead sandwich.

1 Working from front to back, string beads on a headpin to create a bead sandwich. Pull snug so it fits tightly.

2 While maintaining your tension, form a wire-wrapped loop on the back of the sandwich. Before wrapping (finishing) the loop, slip on a large soldered jump ring.

3 Using chainnose pliers, secure two S-hooks to the jump ring, one facing in each direction. Stitch and reinforce a large soldered jump ring to each side of your necklace **(photo a)**: Exit the edging, and pick up about 6–10 small beads. Pick up

the soldered jump ring, and pass back through the first bead. The beads form a loop that holds the jump ring. Pick up another bead, and pass through the edging. Reinforce.

4 Secure an S-hook to the soldered jump ring on one side of the necklace. Use chainnose pliers to close the hook **(photos b and c)**.

Making a shanked button clasp

Use a large button with a shank as your clasp. Embellish the button if desired.

1 Using a jump ring, tightly secure two hooks or S-hooks to the shank, one facing in each direction.

2 Stitch and reinforce a large soldered jump ring to each side of the piece (see above).

3 Attach one of the hooks on the shank to the soldered junmp ring on one side of the necklace. Use chainnose pliers to close the hook completely.

Collar chain clasp

1 Stitch and reinforce a length of chain to each side of the collar, following the instructions for adding soldered jumps rings in step 3 at the top of the page. One length of chain should be about the length of the distance from the edge of the collar to the center of the neck. The other side can be as long as you like.

2 Using chainnose pliers, tightly secure an S-hook or large lobster-claw clasp to the end of the short length of chain.

3 Let the longer chain dangle down the back of the neck, and embellish it as desired.

Finishing with a pin back

1 When you've completed beading your design, knot the thread on the back and trim. Cut around the design as close as possible without cutting any threads.

2 Test the fit of the Ultrasuede on the back of the piece. Identify where the pin back will be placed. Fold the piece of Ultrasuede in half vertically. Position the pin back on the fold **(photo a)**. Locate the stem/joint connection and safety catch on the pin back, and mark their location on the Ultrasuede. Using small scissors, cut a ¼-in. slit where you marked the Ultrasuede. With the pin back open, carefully slide the Ultrasuede over the pin back so that the stem/joint connection and safety catch pass through the cut slits **(photo b)**. Set the Ultrasuede with pin back attached aside.

3 Using a stick, roll a thin, even layer of glue across the entire back surface of the piece. Because the glue will spread when the backing is applied and you still have to pass your needle through those

edges, leave a small unglued margin around the edge. Avoid getting the glue on any part of your pin back or embellishments.

4 Hold the Ultrasuede with the pin back embedded in it so that the stem/joint connection and safety catch are on top and the bar is under the Ultrasuede. Position it above the back of the piece so that the pin back is centered. Press from the inside out to eliminate bumps and air pockets. Take care not to damage your embellishment on the front of the piece. Let the glue dry for at least 20 minutes.

5 Carefully trim the Ultrasuede to match the beadwork. You now have a beadwork/Ultrasuede sandwich **(photo c)**. Edge your work with **blanket stitch edging** or **brick stitch edging (p. 26)**.

6 When you have completed the edging, knot the thread inside the beadwork/Ultrasuede sandwich and trim **(photo c)**.

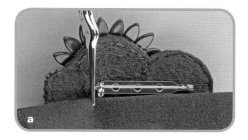

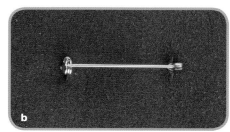

EARRINGS

Attaching an earring wire

1 Holding your earring wire in one hand, grasp one side of the loop with flatnose pliers and gently pull it toward you with chainnose pliers to open **(photo a)**.

2 Slide the component onto the ear wire. To close the loop, grasp the open side of the ear wire loop with the pliers. Push the open side of the loop back until the loop is closed **(photo b)**.

Attaching an earring post

1 Mark the spot where you would like the earring post to sit. The size, shape, and weight of the earring will dictate the post position.

2 Apply E6000 adhesive to the back of your work **(photo a)**.

3 Place the earring post on the position you selected.

4 Make a pinpoint hole in the Ultrasuede. While the glue is still wet, place the Ultrasuede on the back of the cab, pushing the earring post through the pinpoint hole **(photo b)**. Press firmly so that the backing is adhered to the back of the cab. Allow the glue to dry at least 20 minutes. Put the earring back on the post to protect it.

5 Trim **(photo c)** and edge as desired.

Bead Directory

The bead shapes discussed in this book are the most applicable to bead embroidery. There are many other shapes available, and since the theme of this book is "thinking outside the lines," I encourage you to try the others!

Seed Beads

Seed beads are tiny, drawn-glass beads. Most seed beads come in sizes 15º, 11º, 8º, or 6º. Bead sizes are in inverse proportion to the size of the bead. A 15º is almost invisibly tiny, and a 6º is huge. In general, the choice of colors is greatest in 11º.

Due to variations in finish and manufacturing, the actual size of beads varies greatly. Japanese 11ºs, for example, tend to be a little thinner than Czech 11ºs, and a bead with a lot of "effects" on it will be noticeably larger than a bead without effects. For example, the basic transparent 11º will be noticeably smaller than the metallic iris 11º.

Each manufacturer uses a different numbering system for colors, but many of the bead numbers are the same.

Conversely, matching bead colors may be numbered differently for different types of beads within the same manufacturer. And because of the surface area and coatings, the same color can look very different on a 15º and a 6º. When I am working on a piece, I usually try to purchase the same color round seed bead in 15º, 11º, and 8º. That gives me flexibility when trying to balance color in a piece.

Be prepared when shopping for additional beads for an existing project. Stitch samples of each of the beads already in the collection to an index card. For bead colors in multiple sizes, stitch one sample and note the other sizes. If you have a color you want in additional sizes, be sure to jot down the color number. Make a list of what you need right on the card.

Rocaille or round

Rocaille or round seed beads are generally a rounded, almost donut-shaped bead. Czech seed beads are shaped like donuts with rounded edges and small holes. They are usually sold in a hank (12 looped strands of beads tied together at the ends). Their tendency to be irregular in shape and small hole makes them a poor choice for bead weaving, but Czech beads have their place in bead embroidery—if you have the patience to cull them. I especially like to use them as **stop beads (p. 15)**, as they nestle into the primary bead very well.

Japanese seed beads are very different from Czech seed beads. Uniform in size and color, they are typically sold in tubes and are available in a mind-boggling selection of colors. There are three major factories in Japan that produce seed beads: Miyuki, Toho, and Matsuno. Miyuki and Toho beads are a bit more rounded, with large holes. Matsuno beads tend to be taller (hole to hole) than they are around, which makes them look a bit cylindrical.

APPLICATION

Creating cobblestones is a very simple way to add texture. This example uses 6ºs. The technique involves **clustering (p. 21)** 6ºs secured with an 11º stop bead. Try to avoid creating distinct rows. This technique is most effective with random placement, and it is a great way to fill in large areas between elements.

Cylinder seed beads

Cylinder beads (Delica or Aiko) are precision-made, perfectly cylindrical seed beads with polished ends. They have large holes for their size (which accommodate multiple passes of thread), they require little culling, and they come in a huge variety of colors. Ideal for weaving, these uniform seed beads give beadwork a smooth, consistent finish.

These beads are substantially smaller than the same-size round seed beads. Delicas are available in 15°s, 10°s, 11°s, and 8°s, as well as hex cuts. Aikos are available in 11°. Aikos and Delicas are not the same size and will not work together in a woven project.

Cylinder beads do not mesh well together when lined up end to end, and they are not as effective as round seed beads or Charlottes as **stop beads (p. 15)**. Because of their straight sides, they do not nestle into bigger beads, so more thread is visible.

APPLICATION

Cylinders are usually my first choice for bezels, bails, toggles, and closures.

Heavy metal or metal seed beads

Heavy metal or metal beads are brass-based, heavily plated metal beads in a variety of finishes. Very uniform in size with large holes, they are more rounded than Japanese glass beads. The edges of the holes may be sharp and can cut through beading thread. Use Fireline, and avoid pulling or scraping the thread against the edge of the hole. Their color and shine make a strong statement.

APPLICATION

Heavy metal beads can be used in place of seed beads for **backstitching (p. 14)**, **stop beads (p. 15)**, **bezels (p. 17)**, embellishing, and more.

Hexagon or hex

Hexagon or hex beads are six-sided seed beads with rounded holes. They are available in 15°s, 11°s, 8°s, and 6°s in an amazing variety of colors. The Miyuki Delica "cut bead" is also hexagonally shaped. They are generally irregular, sharp, and uneven. Because sharp edges can cut thread, be sure to cull your beads when working with hexes.

APPLICATION

Hex beads can be used with **backstitch (p. 14)** or **stop stitch (p. 15)**. 6° hexes look fabulous stitched upright with a small pearl for the stop bead. You can also use hexes in the **python technique (p. 22)**.

Triangles

Triangles are three-sided beads available in 15°s, 11°s, 8°s, and 6°s. The three-sided triangle bead varies considerably by manufacturer. Toho makes a triangle with crisp corners and a triangular hole. Miyuki makes two varieties of triangle beads. The original was a three-sided bead with rounded edges. They later introduced their "sharp triangles," which are similar to the Toho but with a round hole. Preciosa also makes a triangle bead similar to the original Miyuki, as well as a twisted triangle. Triangles are often imperfectly shaped or broken and require culling.

APPLICATION

Triangles can be used with the **backstitch (p. 14)** or **stop stitch (p. 15)**. My favorite is the **python technique (p. 22)**.

Seed bead drops

There are several kinds of drops with horizontal holes. They have names like drops, fringe beads, magatamas, and tiny tears. The differences are a bit confusing, but they make great texture when used for bead embroidery. They can be **clustered (p. 21)** or used as **stop beads (p. 15)**.

Czech 8º drops are sometimes called tiny tears and are sold in hanks or in tubes. They are an irregular roundish bead with an off-centered hole. Miyuki mini fringe drops are roundish with a centered hole and come in 2.8mm and 3.4mm sizes. These are widely available.

Magatamas are similar to drop beads but they have an off-center hole and are larger, wider and broader in shape. They come in 3mm, 4mm, and 5mm sizes from Toho. Miyuki magatamas are a wider and broader teardrop-shaped bead. They are usually more elongated and less uniform than drop beads.

Long drops are a longer teardrop bead (approximately 6x4mm) with the hole off-centered. These are similar to the Czech 6x4mm teardrops and a little larger than the other Japanese seed bead drops.

Simply bring your thread up where you want your drop to sit, pass through the hole at the bottom of the drop, and pass your thread back down in almost the same point.

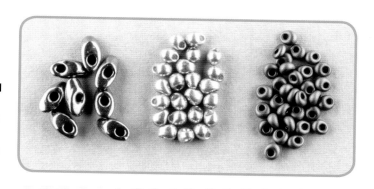

APPLICATION

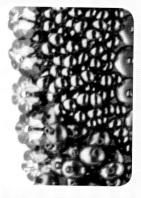

Drop clusters

Drop beads look fabulous tightly clustered together. They are applied without a stop bead. In large patches, they create almost a pebbled effect. You can create designs within the cluster by carefully placing different color drops or different beads in patterns.

Specialty stop bead

Smaller drops work beautifully as a stop bead in a large-hole bead or in a stack stitch. Bring your thread up through the foundation where you want your element to sit. Pick up the large-hole bead and the small drop. Pass your thread back down through the large-hole bead and into the foundation at almost the same point. If the proportions are correct, the base of the small drop will descend into the hole of the large bead and you will see only the rounded top of the drop.

Bugle beads

Bugle beads are long, thin, tubular-shaped beads that are either smooth, twisted, or fluted. They come in sizes from 2–35mm. The length of the bead often influences the diameter of the bead. If you are using Japanese bugles you can usually use them alone, but Czech beads are notorious for their sharp, jagged edges. With any non-Japanese bugles, use a buffer bead (usually an 11º or 15º seed bead) on either end to prevent your thread from breaking. For a monochromatic effect, match the buffer bead to the bugle.

The bugle bead is effective in bead embroidery; however, unless you use very short bugles, work in straight patterns or follow a very gentle curve, it is impossible to apply bugle beads without leaving gaps.

Japanese bugle beads

To stitch a bugle bead, pass up through your foundation, pick up the bugle, and slide the bugle down to the foundation **(figure 1)**. Position the needle immediately adjacent to the edge of the bugle, and pass straight down through the foundation. Bring the needle up immediately adjacent to where you first came up through the foundation, and pass through the bugle again **(figure 2)**. Position the needle immediately adjacent to the bugle, and pass straight down through the foundation. The direction of the bugle is influenced by where you pass back down through the foundation. Move your needle to the next place you want the bugle to sit; repeat.

Czech bugle beads

To stitch a Czech bugle bead, pass up through the foundation and pick up a buffer bead, the bugle bead, and a second buffer bead **(figure 3)**. Position your needle immediately adjacent to the second buffer bead and pass straight down through the foundation. Bring the needle up immediately adjacent to the first buffer bead, and pass through all three beads again. Position the needle immediately adjacent to the second buffer bead and pass straight down through the foundation. The direction of the bugle is influenced by where you pass back down through the foundation. Move your needle to the next place you want the bugle to sit, and repeat **(figure 4)**.

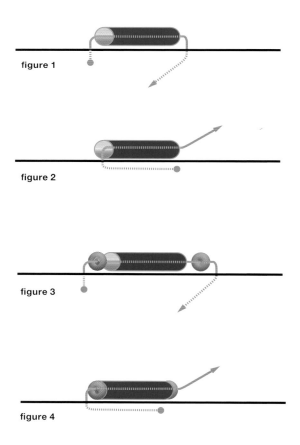

figure 1

figure 2

figure 3

figure 4

APPLICATION

figure 1

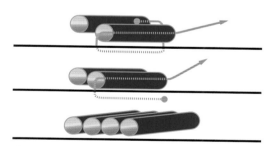

figure 2

End-to-end

Stitch bugle beads end to end to create lines **(figure 1)**. Where you bring your thread back down through the foundation determines the direction of your line. Stick to gentle curves. If you stitch them at too sharp an angle, you will see the thread and the hole edge of the bead.

Side-by-side

Line bugle beads up vertically side by side to create "blocks" or vertical lines of bugles (like a long wooden fence) **(figure 2)**. By making tiny adjustments to the spaces between the beads, you can make gentle curves. If you separate the top of the beads, it will curve one way; separating the bottom makes it curve in the opposite direction.

Charlottes (one-cuts)

A Charlotte is a seed bead with a single facet hand ground into each bead. These beads are available in 8°s, 11°s, 13°s, and 15°s. They have subtle sparkle. 13° Czech Charlottes are widely available and are effective in **backstitch (p. 14)**, but 15°s are best as **stop beads (p. 15)**. The Japanese Charlotte, available in 12°s and 15°s, is a relative newcomer.

APPLICATION

My favorites for stop beads are 15° Charlottes. They are tiny and nestle nicely into most beads. 15°s are a great choice for the final row of a **bezel (p. 17)**. 13° Charlottes are effective in **backstitch (p. 14)**.

Czech Pressed Glass

Czech beads (also known as pressed glass beads) can be found in an incredible variety of shapes, colors, and finishes. For starters there are rounds, ovals, daggers, drops, lentils, rondelles, leaves, flowers, cubes, disks, squares and diamonds. There are even jalapeños, cherries, citrus fruits, and grapes! Shapes introduced in the last few years include spikes, studs, pyramids, gumdrops, rizos, O beads, and Czech Mates (various shapes with two holes).

Colors and finishes include transparent, opaque, matte, iris, AB, opal, alabaster, atlas, and silk. Then they are painted, dipped, sprayed, or encased in metal coatings. The most exciting Czech glass finish is the peacock. The original peacock bead sported large iridescent polka dots that looked like the "eye" spots on peacock feathers. The effect is produced by applying a coating using a stencil. The beads

are now available with many different patterns and shapes including triangles, squares, stripes, tie-dye, and grids.

There are quite a few shapes that you can use in textured bead embroidery.

Fire-polished beads

Fire-polished beads come in every shape imaginable (round, bicone, drop, rondelle, etc.), but rounds are most common and have the greatest availability of colors and finishes. They are available in a wide variety of transparent, opaque, metallic, Picasso and AB (Aurora Borealis) colors. While they are sold in sizes from 2–20mm, the greatest color selection is in 4mm and 6mm. A "round" fire-polished bead is actually more of an oblong shape than a true sphere.

APPLICATION

Use 6–8mm fire-polished rondelles (donut-shaped) with a **stop bead (p. 15)** to add sparkle. Unique matte metallic fire-polished beads also add texture and interest.

TIP: Some beads have shape direction. For example, a flat drop may have a curved tip. Keep this in perspective when you are stitching these beads. If you are doing a uniform border, you do not want a rogue bead facing in the wrong direction.

TIP: Many Czech glass finishes are applied only to one side. When you are working with these beads, make sure the color you want is facing in the right direction. I use beads with the finish on one side only in both directions for additional texture and interest.

Glass drops

Pressed glass drops (usually Czech) are more drop-shaped and come in a variety of sizes with 6x4mm as the most commonly available. Vertical drops (usually Czech) are a slightly more elongated drop with the hole running from top to bottom.

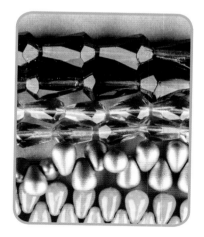

APPLICATION

Cabochon embellishment

Drops are great for embellishing cabochons using the **stitch-in-the-ditch technique (p. 19)**. To make them stand up, stitch an 11º seed bead between each drop: With the needle exiting the hole in the drop, pick up an 11º, and pass through the next drop. Repeat until there is a 11º between each drop.

Pass the needle through both the drops and the 11ºs at least one more time. Use a little tension if you want the drops to stand up. To maintain the tension, work your thread down into the foundation, pull tight, and make several **half-hitch knots (p. 13)** while you are still pulling on the thread.

Round or druk

Druks are smooth, round, pressed-glass beads imported from the Czech Republic. Like fire-polished beads, they are available in a wide variety of transparent, opaque, metallic, Picasso and AB (Aurora Borealis) colors. While they are sold in sizes from 3–20mm, the greatest color selection is in 4mm and 6mm. Although they are called round, if you look closely, they are not truly a sphere. They tend to be longer in the direction of the drilled hole than they are wide. It is not unusual for the drill channel to be visible in transparent druks.

APPLICATION

Smaller (3mm and 4mm) sizes can be sewn using **backstitch (p. 14)**, as a **stop bead (p. 15)**, in **clusters** sewn with a stop bead **(p. 21)**, used to embellish a cabochon by **stitching in the ditch (p. 19)**, and in **stack stitches** on top of a rondelle or other disk-shaped bead **(p. 15)**.

Use larger (6mm and 8mm) sizes as accent beads stitched with stop beads or in a stack stitch.

Daggers

Dagger (sometimes called spears) beads are long, flat pressed glass beads that resemble daggers, flower petals, or dragonfly wings. They start out narrow at the base and flare out to a wider, almost rounded top, usually with a little peak at the top. They are drilled laterally through the base.

They come in many different colors and finishes. Common sizes are 16x5mm and 10x3mm (some call it 11x3mm). Harder to find are 14x7mm "fat" daggers and 9x3mm "baby daggers." Anything bigger tends to be cumbersome for bead embroidery.

Daggers create texture regardless of how you use them, but I love them most tightly clustered together in a **dagger cluster:** Bring your thread up through the foundation where you want your dagger to sit, pass through the hole at the bottom of the dagger, and pass the thread down into the foundation at almost the same point **(figure 1)**. To give your dagger a little extra support, bring the thread up through the foundation where you want your dagger to sit, pick up a seed bead, and pass through the hole at the bottom of the dagger. Pick up another seed bead, and pass the thread down into the foundation at almost the same point **(figure 2)**.

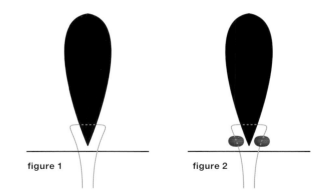

figure 1   figure 2

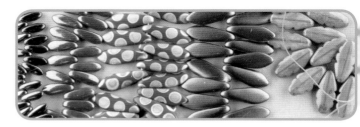

Dagger row

1 Bring the thread up through the foundation where you want your dagger to sit, pass through the hole at the bottom of the dagger, and pass the thread down through the foundation at almost the same point **(figure 1)**.

2 Bring the needle up against the dagger where you first brought up your thread, and pass through the dagger again. Pick up another dagger and slide it against the original dagger. Position the needle immediately adjacent to the new dagger, and pass straight down through the foundation **(figure 2)**. Bring your needle up between the first and second dagger, and pass through the newest dagger again **(figure 3)**. Repeat **(figure 4)** until you are satisfied with the element.

3 To help the daggers stand up in an embellishment, you can stitch an 8° or 11° seed between each dagger **(figure 5)**. (Try a hex or triangle bead for more interest and texture.)

4 Reinforce and connect the daggers by passing through the holes at least one more time.

5 Use a **support row (p. 23)** to influence the slope of your daggers (the bigger the support bead, the deeper the tilt).

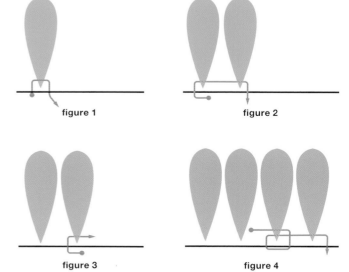

figure 1   figure 2

figure 3   figure 4

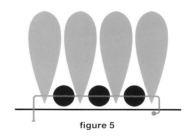

figure 5

APPLICATION

Embellishing a cabochon with daggers

One of my favorite ways to create excitement in a piece is to embellish a cabochon with daggers. The beautiful spears lie horizontally, fanning out around the focal like the rays of the sun or the petals of a flower.

1 Bring your thread up through the foundation at the edge of your bezel. Pass through the beads in the bezel (make sure your thread does not show) until you reach the row where you want your dagger to sit. Pick up a dagger, and pass the thread through the next bead in the same row. Pick up another dagger, and pass your thread through the next bead in the same row. Continue until you have added all of the daggers.

2 Step up through the first dagger in the row. For added support, stitch a decorative bead between each dagger. Reinforce the daggers with another thread pass. Secure and trim the thread.

3 If the daggers droop, add a support row before securing and trimming your thread. Move your thread to the row of the bezel behind your daggers. Use the **stitch-in-the-ditch technique (p. 19)** to add a line of seed beads to this row.

Want your daggers to angle up? Before securing and trimming your thread, move your thread to the row of the bezel behind your daggers. Use the stitch-in-the-ditch technique to add a line of small drops or druks to the row of the bezel behind your daggers. Rule of thumb: the bigger the support bead, the deeper the tilt of the daggers.

4 You can also embellish with more than one row of daggers, or maybe two different size daggers. Before securing and trimming your thread, move your thread to the row of the bezel above your daggers. Use the stitch-in-the-ditch technique to add another line of daggers (make sure you position the daggers correctly above the first row).

5 If your daggers refuse to cooperate, use the heaviest thread that will pass easily through the beads. Pull gently but securely. Without releasing the tension on your thread, tie a **half-hitch knot (p. 13)**. Pass through the next dagger and the next bezel bead (tugging the knot inside the dagger), and tie another half-hitch knot. Repeat for each dagger. Knot and trim your thread.

Rizos

Rizos are small (2.5x6mm) drop beads shaped like a grain of rice. They are smaller than a baby dagger, but thinner and more uniformly shaped than a Japanese drop or magatama. The hole is at one end, making them perfect for bead embroidery.

APPLICATION

Use Rizos in **clusters (p. 21)** or as embellishments.

Rondelles, heishi, or disk

Rondelles are small, usually flat round beads with a hole in the center. This shape is also known as a heishi, wheel, donut, wafer, or spacer bead. They are available in a variety of sizes and have a ton of possibilities. Bring your thread up where you want your rondelle to sit, and pass through the hole in the middle of the rondelle. Pick up a stop bead, and pass your thread back down through the rondelle only in almost the same point **(figure 1)**. Pull snug **(figure 2)**.

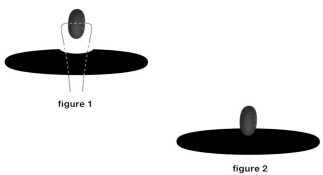

figure 1

figure 2

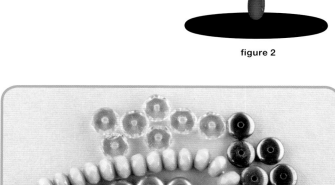

APPLICATION

Rondelles are excellent for layering in **stack stitches (p. 15)**. They are thin and flat, and work well to support other beads. For example, make a bead sandwich with a rondelle, a 4mm druk, and a 15º Charlotte.

Emphasize the flow of your project by stitching a meandering trail of rondelles using the **stop stitch (p. 15)** or stack stitch. Use rondelles and 15º seed beads. Position the next rondelle immediately adjacent to the first, but following your predetermined path. Keep stitching rondelles until you come to the end of the trail.

Tadpoles (pendants)

These are one of my favorite beads. I have only found them in a few places. Beadcats.com calls them "Pendants." Fusionbeads.com calls them "Flat drop with curved tip." I call them tadpoles because that is what they look like to me. A tadpole is basically a 9x5mm flat pointed bead that is rounded at the top (the location of the hole) with a curved tip. The hole is oriented back to front.

APPLICATION

Use tadpoles in **clusters (p. 21)**, placing the beads randomly for a messy, stacked effect.

Lentils and Oval Lentils

Lentils are disk-shaped beads, similar to rondelles, except that the hole is near one edge. There are two basic ways to apply lentils: To stand them on one edge, bring your thread up where you want your lentil to sit, pass through the hole, and then pass your thread back down through the foundation at almost the same point. Pull snug **(figures 1 and 2)**. To stitch them flat or at a slight angle, bring your thread up where you want your lentil to sit, and pass through the lentil. Pick up a stop bead, and pass your thread back down through the lentil in almost the same point. Pull snug **(figures 3 and 4)**.

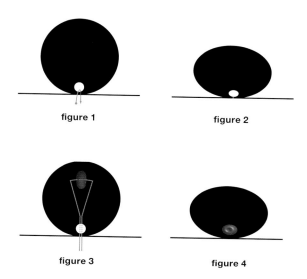

figure 1

figure 2

figure 3

figure 4

APPLICATION

Lentil cluster

Lentil clusters work best when worked using a stop bead. Use an 11º stop bead if you want more texture or a 15º if you want the lentil to be the star. Choose a contrasting color for greater impact or a matching color for a more subtle look. Follow the general directions for a **cluster** with a stop bead **(p. 15)**. Make sure that each lentil is positioned right against

the previous lentil. Twist the lentils so they face in different directions to achieve the maximum texture.

Shields (pendants)

These wonderful beads are as elusive as the tadpoles. Beadcats.com calls them "Pendants." Fusionbeads.com calls them "Flat-pointed drops." I think they look like a knight's shield. These beads are 10x5mm, flat at the top (the location of the hole), flare out at the sides, and come to a point at the tip. The hole is also oriented from back to front.

APPLICATION

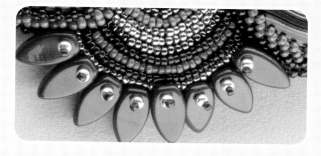

Shield embellishment

To use the shields as an embellishment suspended over the edge of a pendant, bring your thread up where you want your shield to sit, and pass through the shield. Pick up a **stop bead (p. 15)**, and pass your thread back down through the shield in almost the same point. Pull snug. You can also apply shields in **clusters (p. 21)**.

Spikes

A relative newcomer to the bead market, the Czech glass spike is a wonderful cone-shaped bead with a wide base that tapers to a pointed end. The hole is usually drilled through the widest portion of the cone. It is available in three sizes: 18x12mm, 17x7mm, and 8x5mm.

APPLICATION

Spike row

1 Bring your thread up through the foundation where you want your spike to sit, pass through the hole at the bottom of the spike, and then pass your needle straight down into the foundation where your thread exits the hole on the other side.

2 Bring the needle up against the spike where you first brought up the thread, and pass through the spike again. Pick up another spike and slide it against the original spike.

3 Position your needle immediately adjacent to the new spike, and pass straight down through the foundation. Bring your needle up between the first and second spike, and pass through the newest spike again.

4 Repeat as desired. To help the spikes stand up in an embellishment, you may stitch an 8º or 11º seed between each spike. Reinforce and connect the spikes by passing through them one more time. Knot and trim your thread.

Embellishing a cabochon with spikes

1 Pass through the beads in the bezel until you reach the row where you want your spike to sit **(photo a)**. Pick up a spike, and pass through the next bead in the same bezel row **(photo b)**. You may have to skip every-other bead, depending on the size of the spike. Pick up another spike, and pass the thread through the next bead in the same row. Continue as desired **(photo c)**.

2 To hide the thread between the spikes, stitch a small (2–3mm) round bead between each spike **(photo d)**. If the spikes are not being stitched completely around the bezel (like in the photos here), follow the instructions for stitching the spikes on the "Spineless Earrings" (see p. 71) to add a small round bead on the ends of the spike section. If there is room in the beads, reinforce the spikes with another thread pass. Knot and trim your thread.

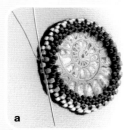

a

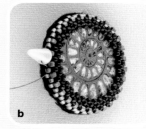

b

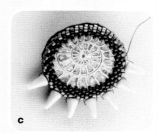

c

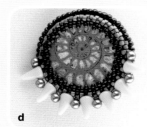

d

PEARLS

Pearls come in a wonderful variety of shapes, sizes, and colors.

Round pearls

Except for the finest-quality pearls, natural round pearls are never actually round. In addition, they generally have a very fine hole, sometimes making it difficult to pass through with a needle and thread even one time. For the purposes of bead embroidery, the slightly oblong or irregular shape of the natural round pearl is not an issue. Glass pearls are man-made objects designed to resemble real pearls. A glass bead is dipped or sprayed with pearlescent material, which imitates the natural iridescence of a pearl. The resulting pearl is usually uniform in size and shape. Before using glass pearls in your work, I recommend that you test the finish. Check to see if the color rubs off, and make sure that the finish is not peeling at the hole. Crystal pearls are a dream come true for bead embroidery. Their uniform shape, broad range of colors, durable coating, and large holes facilitate almost anything you would want to do with a pearl. Swarovski also manufactures baroque, twist, and drop-shaped pearls. While the shapes are interesting, they are too large for most bead embroidery.

APPLICATION

Round pearls cluster

The round pearl cluster is most effective with smaller pearls (5mm or less). Create a **cluster (p. 21)** using seed beads as stop beads. Don't place the pearls in rows; You want it to look like you spilled a pile of pearls. For added texture, allow the pearls to overlap each other. Stitch the initial layer of tightly clustered pearls. Randomly fill in the spaces between the pearls with more pearls. For more height, keep adding layers.

Round pearl row

1 Bring your thread up through the foundation where you want your pearl to sit, pass through the hole in the pearl, and pass your thread down into the foundation at almost the same point.

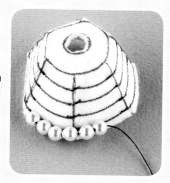

2 Bring your needle up against the pearl where you first brought up your thread, and pass through the pearl again. Pick up another pearl, and slide it against the original pearl. Position your needle immediately adjacent to the new pearl, and pass straight down through the foundation. Bring your needle up between the first and second pearl, and pass through the newest pearl again.

3 Repeat this process until you are satisfied with the element. Reinforce and connect the pearls by passing through the holes at least one more time if possible. You may want fill in between the round pearls with a seed bead combination, such as a 15º sitting on top of an 11º.

Keishi pearls

Keishi pearls are small, irregular (deformed) pearls. Keishi pearls come in an array of colors, and tend to have a high luster and shimmering surface quality. There are several forms of keishi pearls: Biwa pearls, also called stick pearls, are long, flat and narrow; baroque pearls are pear-shaped with an odd tip; and coin pearls are traditionally disk-shaped pearls. The term keishi most commonly refers to petal, flake, or cornflake-shaped pearls.

Typically, pearls are drilled from top to bottom, from side to side, or through the narrowest end at the top of the pearl.

APPLICATION

Mermaid tail

The mermaid tail uses center-drilled keishi or cornflake pearls, the larger and more concave (or bowl-shaped), the better. The mermaid tail layers cornflake pearls in casual rows following the contour of the work. Think of fish scales—or a mermaid's tail.

1 Pass up through the foundation in the exact spot you wish the pearl to sit. Pick up a keishi pearl and a 15º seed bead. Skip the 15º, and pass down through the keishi pearl and foundation.

2 Approximate where the center of the pearl should sit in order for the next keishi to be positioned right against the first (slightly overlapping). Pass up through the foundation at that center point.

3 Pick up the keishi pearl and a 15º. Skip the 15º, and pass down through the keishi pearl and foundation. Pull tightly so that the pearls cluster together.

4 Making sure the tops of the pearls face in the same direction, continue layering the pearls in short rows until you achieved the look you want.

SEMIPRECIOUS STONES

In most cases, my cabochons are some variety of semiprecious stone. When possible, I like to use matching or coordinating small shapes in other areas of the piece for balance and interest. Depending on the shape, they are applied with backstitch or stop stitch.

APPLICATION

The shape of a semi-precious stone dictates its application. Use the guidelines for similar shapes in glass beads.

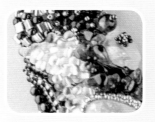

Chips or nuggets

Gemstone chips are small irregularly-shaped tumbled stone beads that are strung sideways. They are thinner, smaller, or flatter than their big brother, the nugget bead. They are available in a variety of sizes, typically with a smooth finish and somewhat rounded edges. Chips on the same strand will vary in size by a few millimeters. For bead embroidery, I choose the smallest chips I can find. Larger pieces are clunky and heavy.

APPLICATION

Chip cluster

Create a **cluster (p. 21)** using seed beads as stop beads. Do not place the chips in rows; you want it to look like you spilled a pile of chips. For added texture and dimension, allow the chips to overlap each other. Stitch the initial layer of tightly clustered chips. Randomly fill in the spaces between the chips with more chips. For more height, keep adding layers.

Faceted gemstone teardrops or briolettes

Teardrops and briolette beads are classic shapes for beadwork. A briolette is an elongated pear-shaped gemstone cut in long triangular facets, usually with a pointed end drilled at the top. Briolette cuts are found in almost all gemstones. A teardrop is exactly what it sounds like: anything shaped like a falling drop.

APPLICATION

Pass up through the foundation in the exact spot you wish the element to sit. Pick up the teardrop/briolette and pass down through the foundation. They are most effective in clusters, as fans or as embellishments. Be very careful when using these beads. They have a tendency to cut your thread, so use Fireline 10 lb. test.

OTHER ELEMENTS

Crystals

There are countless shapes, colors, and sizes of crystals—and new ones keep coming. While Swarovski has been the gold standard in crystal for many years, the Czech Preciosa line is rapidly expanding with a slightly better price point.

Keep in mind that the hole of any true crystal may have sharp edges. Always use a heavier thread and take care not to pull your thread against the edge of the hole—pull in the direction of the hole. There are rounds, bicones, drops, rings, and triangles. One of my favorite crystal beads is the margarita, a lovely flower shape with many uses in bead embroidery.

APPLICATION

Let the shape and size of your crystal dictate its application. For example, rounds can be used in place of any round bead. You can also use many of the methods for applying round beads for bicone beads—you just get a little more sparkle. I frequently use crystals with **stop beads** as an embellishment or in a **stack stitch (p. 15)**.

Branch beads

A branch is a narrow, irregular shape that twists and curves like a tree branch or a branch of coral. Branches are usually lightweight and add tremendous interest to a piece.

APPLICATION

The branch is most effective in a **cluster (p. 21)**, especially when you allow the branches to extend over the edge of another component. Although a stop bead is not necessary, you can add interest and reduce the risk of visible thread by using a 15º or Charlotte **stop bead (p. 15)**.

Projects

Ilien
pendant

With tassels and crystals on the brain, this design materialized as I was sketching to pass the time on an airplane (where I do my best work). Instead of suspending this pendant from bubble chain as directed, consider stitching a coordinating rope.

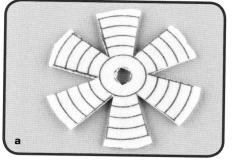

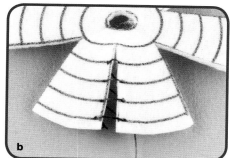

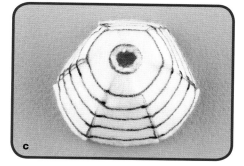

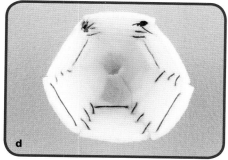

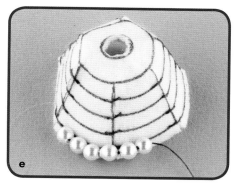

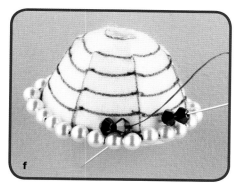

Materials

- 14mm crystal cosmic triangle
- 12mm large-hole crystal pearl
- 8mm round crystal bead
- **46** 7mm small crystal briolette pendants
- 4mm bicone crystals
  25–30 color A
  25–30 color B
  20–25 color C
- 3mm crystal pearls
  25–30 color D
  25–30 color E
  20–25 color F
- 1g 8º hex beads
- 1g 8º triangle beads
- 1g 15º Charlottes
- 16 ft. bubbles or other decorative chain (www.primitiveearthbeads.com)
- 10 in. 24-gauge craft wire
- **2** 5mm 18-gauge jump rings
- **46** 4mm 24-gauge jump rings
- clasp
- beading foundation
- Fireline, 10 lb. test
- Fireline, 8 lb. test

Tools

- beading needles, #12 and #13
- scissors and embroidery scissors
- pencil or similar dowel shape
- chainnose pliers
- roundnose pliers
- flush cutters

Constructing the dome

1 Transfer the dome pattern to your beading foundation **(CD or pattern, p. 55)**.

2 Leaving a ⅛-in. margin, cut out the pattern. Cut out and discard the six orange checkered triangles. To remove the orange checkered circle at the center, carefully poke small embroidery scissors through the center and cut around the edge. Your pattern will now resemble a ceiling fan with six paddles **(photo a)**.

3 Thread a needle with a comfortable length of 10 lb. test thread, and knot the end. Pull two of the paddles together so that the lines match up. Bring the needle up from the back on the lowest line of the left paddle, approximately ⅛ in. from the right edge. Bring the needle down

through the lowest line of the right paddle ⅛ in. from the left edge. Pull gently so that the lines match up and meet. (If you pull too hard, the dome will pucker.) Bring the needle up from the back on the next line of the left paddle ⅛ in. from the right edge. Bring the needle down through the matching line of the right paddle ⅛ in. from the left edge. Pull so the lines match up and meet. Repeat two more times **(photo b)**.

4 Draw the next paddle to the two that are now connected. From the back, move your needle to the next seam and come up on the fourth line ⅛ in. from the right edge. Now working down, work as in steps 3 and 4. Continue in this fashion until all six paddles are connected to form a small dome. Keep your tension firm but relaxed so the paddles stay

together but the dome does not pucker. Secure and trim the thread **(photos c and d)**.

Embellishing the dome

1 Thread a needle with a comfortable length of 8 lb. test thread, and knot the end. Starting on the lowest line in the middle of a paddle, **backstitch (p. 14)** a row of 3mm color D pearls on the line **(photo e)**. As you add rows of beads, tension will cause the ⅛-in. margin to roll into the dome, and these pearls become

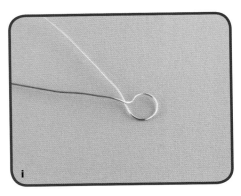

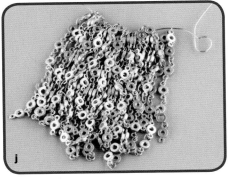

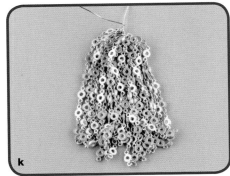

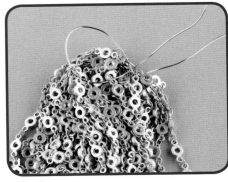

the finished edge. From here on, the lines on the foundation are only there as a guide to keeping your rows straight. The previous row will determine the placement of subsequent rows.

2 Backstitch a row of 4mm color A bicone crystals above the pearls so the bicones fill in the gaps between the pearls **(photo f)**.

3 Using **stop stitch (p. 15)**, add a row of 8º hex beads secured with 15º Charlotte seed beads. Position the hexes so they fill in the V-shaped spaces above the As **(photo g)**.

4 Backstitch a row of 4mm color B bicone crystals to fill in the V-shaped spaces above the hexes.

5 Backstitch a row of 3mm color E pearls so they fill in the V-shaped spaces above the bicones.

6 Using stop stitch, add a row of 8º triangle beads secured with 15ºs.

7 Backstitch a row of 3mm color F pearls against the triangles.

8 Backstitch a row of 4mm color C bicone crystals against the pearls so they fill in the gaps between the pearls **(photo h)**.

9 Secure and trim the thread. Set the dome aside.

Making the tassel

The design of your gold chain will be a factor in the length of your tassel. Because of the pattern sequence in the chain, each strand of my chain is seven "bubbles" (about 2½ in.) long. Between each "bubble" is a thin link. The lengths of chain will be suspended from these links.

1 Using a 10-in. length of craft wire, create the initial loop for a wire wrap about the diameter of a pencil **(photo i)**. You will create the tassel with three different lengths of folded chain. To start, count seven bubbles and slide the link between the seventh and eighth bubbles onto your wire wrap. Count 14 bubbles and slide the link between the 14th and 15th bubbles onto your wire wrap. (Later, you will clip the link between the seventh and eighth bubbles so that each strand has seven bubbles.) Continue counting 14 bubbles and adding the link 11 more times. Count seven more bubbles and cut the link. Slide everything into the initial loop. This represents 26 strands of your tassel **(photo j)**.

2 Holding the initial loop (without crushing your chain), wrap one tail of the wire around the base of the loop one full revolution **(photo k)**.

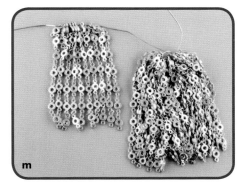

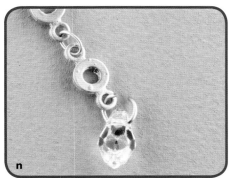

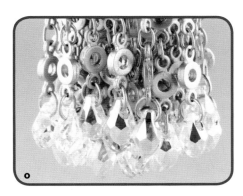

3 On one side of the wrap, count seven bubbles and slide the link between the seventh and eighth bubbles onto your wire wrap. Count 14 bubbles and slide the link between the 14th and 15th bubbles onto your wire wrap. Repeat three more times. Count seven more bubbles and cut the link. Slide the lengths of chain against the previous cluster, and bring the wire tail through the initial loop. Using chainnose pliers, pull the loop tightly. This represents 10 more strands of the tassel **(photo l)**.

4 Work as in step 3 with the other side of the wrap **(photo m)**.

5 Bring both tails of the wire up so they are now parallel, and trim to the same length.

6 Separate the still-connected chains into individual strands by clipping the small links between them at the bottom. When finished, each strand will include seven bubbles.

7 Attach a 7mm briolette to the bottom of each strand of the tassel using a 4mm jump ring **(photos n and o)**.

Assembly

1 Slide both tassel wires through the dome from bottom to top. Slide a 12mm large-hole pearl, a 14mm cosmic triangle, and a 8mm round crystal on the wires **(photo p)**. Pull firmly. The pearl should recess slightly into the row of crystals at the top of the dome. If it does not, use chainnose pliers to gently pull the wires taut (take care not to break your wire or chain).

2 Wrap the wires to create a bail at the top of the tassel **(photo q)**.

3 Double the remaining 60 in. of chain. Using a 5mm jump ring, attach the pair of end links to one side of the clasp. Slide the tassel on the chain. Clip the small link connecting the two strands of chain at the other end, and connect both end links to the other side of the clasp using another 5mm jump ring **(photo r)**.

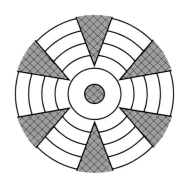

pattern

Rosie
pendant

Rosie was inspired by two little cabochons with a remarkable story. They are called fordite, also known as motor agate, a by-product of the now extinct practice of hand spray-painting cars in factories. Colorful layers of enamel paint overspray gradually built up on the metal racks that transported car bodies through the paint shop and into ovens where each coat was baked. Auto workers with vision chipped out the hardened material, and fordite was born.

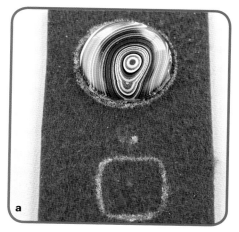

Materials

- 30mm cabochon with distinctive geometric pattern
- 20–25mm matching smaller cabochon, preferably in a different shape
- **4–5** 14x7mm "fat" peacock dagger beads
- **8–10** Czech glass shields
- 4mm druk or 6º seed bead
- **7–10** 3.4mm drops
- **8–10** 8º seed beads (heavy metal)
- 1g 11º seed beads in **2** colors
- 1g 15º seed beads in **4** colors
- 1g 15º Charlotte seed beads in **2** colors
- Fireline, 8 lb. test
- Ultrasuede
- E6000 adhesive
- 4x5 in. beading foundation
- ½-in.-wide Terrifically Tacky Tape

Tools

- beading needles, #12 and #13
- scissors
- embroidery scissors
- chalk or permanent marker

Making the pin

Note: Because the methods that created fordite have been obsolete since the late seventies, it is hard to find and a bit pricey. You can substitute any cabochon with a distinct repetitive pattern that can be reproduced with rows of backstitched beads.

1 Position the large and small cabochons on your beading foundation about ¾ in. apart. (You may want to alter this distance if your cabs are smaller or larger. The distance should be three-quarters of the size of the large cab.) Trace around the cabs with chalk or a permanent marker to create your pattern. Set the cabs aside.

2 Mark a point centered ¼ in. above the small cab (or one-quarter of the size of the large cab) **(photo a)**.

3 Adhere the large cab to the beading foundation using Terrifically Tacky Tape, thread a needle with a comfortable length of thread, and **bezel the cab (p. 17),** starting with an 11º seed bead and decreasing to a 15º seed bead. The number of rows needed will be determined by the height of the cab, the size of the beads, and the tension of your work. Once you have finished the bezel, secure and trim the thread.

4 Repeat steps 2 and 3 with the small cab, using a different combination of colors **(photo b)**.

5 Using **stop stitch (p. 15)**, attach a 4mm druk or 6º seed bead with a 15º Charlotte stop bead at the point you marked ¼ in. above the small cab. Using 15ºs, **backstitch (p. 14)** a series of tight, concentric circles around the druk, alternating the four colors **(photo c)**.

6 After a few rows, the circles will "dead end" into the smaller cab, and a few rows later, the circles will be obstructed by the larger cab. Backstitch circles on either side of the cabs, following the imaginary line through the cab. Let the preceding backstitch rows guide you.

7 Continue until the circles extend about one-half of the way down the smaller cab. Secure and trim the thread.

8 Stitch a **cluster (p. 21)** of five 3.4mm drop beads to the left of the small cab at its approximate center **(photo d)**.

9 On the left side of the larger cab, stitch a **dagger row (p. 42)** of four or five 16x5mm daggers.

10 Bring the thread up immediately adjacent to the outside of the uppermost dagger, and pass through the uppermost dagger. Stitch an 11º (in a contrasting color to the daggers) between each of the daggers in the first row. When you have passed through the lowest dagger, pick up an 11º and a 15º. Pass back through the 11º and through the lowest dagger, pulling snug. Continue to pass through all of the daggers and separating seed beads. After you have passed through the lowest dagger, pick up an 11º and a 15º. Pass back through the 11º and through the lowest dagger, pulling snug **(photo e)**. Secure and trim your thread.

11 Following the curve on the right side of the backstitched concentric circles, stitch Czech shield beads using a combination of 8º seed beads and 15º Charlottes as stop beads **(photos f and g)**.

Finishing

1 Cut around your design as close as possible without cutting any threads. Trim under the daggers and the shield beads so they extend beyond the foundation **(photos h and i)**.

2 Apply backing (p. 25) to the back of your beadwork using Ultrasuede. Take care not to damage the embellishment on the front of the cab. Let the glue dry for at least 20 minutes.

3 Trim the Ultrasuede to match the beadwork. You now have a beadwork/ Ultrasuede sandwich. Again, trim under the daggers and the shield beads so they extend beyond the foundation/ Ultrasuede sandwich.

4 Edge the work with **blanket stitch edging (p. 26)** using the 11ºs. Note that the edging is sewn under the daggers and shields. When you have completed the edging, knot the thread inside the beadwork/Ultrasuede sandwich and trim.

Making the bail

Complete the bail with **odd-count flat peyote stitch (p. 16)**, working off the bezel and the edging of your work:

1 Find the center of the top of the bezel on the large cabochon. Working on the second row of the bezel, count two beads to the left of center. Start a thread, and exit the second bead to the left of center, working from left to right. Work four peyote stitches using 11⁰s in the color matching that row of the bezel. Turn around and work three peyote stitches **(photos j and k)**.

2 Still using odd-count peyote stitch, stitch a total of 18 rows. Lock in the last bead on the final row: Turn, and pass through the first two beads in the row immediately below where your thread is exiting **(photo l)**. Turn, and pass through the two beads immediately above where your thread is exiting. Your thread has now returned to its original location, but you have secured that last bead. This will keep it in place as you complete the bail **(photo m)**.

3 Fold the bail toward the back of the cab. Follow the thread path to "zip" the edge of the bail to the first row of the bezel. Reinforce **(photo n)**.

4 Embellish the edges of the bail with 15⁰s by **blanket stitching (p. 26)** through the threads on the edges of the bail **(photo o)**. Secure the thread.

Tiny Dancer
pendant

This project is a perfect example of what happens when you let the beads "do their thing." I loved the fabulous colors and unusual shape of this cabochon (which is somewhere between a pear and a drop). When I searched through my stash to see what worked with its colors, I discovered these delicious marquise-shaped patinated drops and tiny pearls. I just let the beads take the lead, and I love the result.

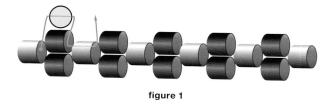

figure 1

figure 2

Materials

- Narrow pear or drop-shaped cabochon
- **40–50** 26x11mm patinated marquise-shaped brass drops in **2** or **3** colors (www.firemountaingems.com)
- **40–50** 2mm Czech glass pearls
- 2g 11º seed beads
- 2g 15º seed beads
- Fireline, 8 lb. test
- 4x5-in. piece of beading foundation
- Ultrasuede
- E6000 adhesive
- ½-in. wide Terrifically Tacky Tape

Tools

- beading needles, #12
- scissors
- embroidery scissors

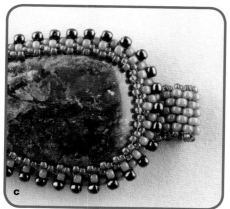

Making the pendant

1 Adhere the cabochon to the beading foundation using Terrifically Tacky Tape, thread a needle with a comfortable single-strand length of thread, and **bezel the cab (p. 17)**, starting with 11º seed beads and decreasing to two or three rows of 15º seed beads in a contrasting color. Once you have finished the bezel, secure and trim the thread **(photo a)**.

2 Starting a new thread and using the **stitch-in-the-ditch technique (p. 19)**, stitch a 2mm pearl between each of the beads in the second row of 11ºs **(figures 1 and 2)**. Secure and trim the thread.

Making the bail

1 Cut around your design as close as possible without cutting any threads.

2 Using 11ºs and working off the first bezel row of 11ºs, stitch a five-bead-wide (three beads on one row and two beads on the next) 16-row bail in **odd-count flat peyote stitch (p. 16)**. Zip the bail to the first bezel row **(photo b)**.

3 Embellish the edges of the bail with **whipstitch edging (p. 21)** using 15ºs through the beads on the edges of the bail **(photos c and d)**. Secure the thread.

Finishing

1 Apply backing (p. 25) to your beadwork using Ultrasuede. Let the glue dry for at least 20 minutes.

2 Carefully trim the Ultrasuede to match the beadwork. Edge your work with **blanket stitch edging (p. 26)** using 15°s.

3 Once you have completed the edging, knot the thread inside the beadwork/Ultrasuede sandwich, and trim **(photo e)**.

Adding fringe

1 Add fringe off the beads on the lowest quarter of the bezeled cab only. To begin, thread a needle and knot. Using the pearls as a reference, identify the first edge bead on the lower quarter of the cab. Hide the thread under the bezel beads and bring the needle through the first edge bead, pointing toward the bottom of the cab.

2 Pick up two 11°s, three 15°s, a marquise drop, and three 15°s. (The drops I used have a gold edge on one side only. For a uniform look, pick up the drops in the same direction each time.) Pass up through the two 11°s, and pull the fringe so that no thread is showing but it is relaxed enough to drape nicely. Pass back through the original edge bead from the same direction pointing toward the bottom, and pass through the edge bead immediately adjacent to the first edge bead **(figure 3)**.

3 Repeat the previous step for each edge bead on the lower quarter of the cab, alternating the colors of the drops **(figures 4 and 5)**.

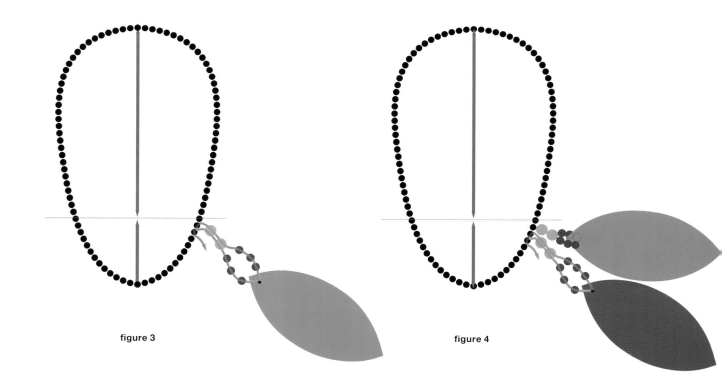

figure 3

figure 4

4 The next line of fringe will be worked off the 11°s in the bezel, alternating between rows one and two. Move your thread up to the cylinder bead in the second row of the bezel (the same row as the pearls) even with the first fringed edge bead, working toward the bottom of the cab **(figure 6)**.

5 Pick up two 11°s, three 15°s, a drop, and three 15°s. Pass back up through the two 11°s, and pull the fringe so that no thread is showing, but it is relaxed enough to drape nicely. Pass back through the 11° your thread is exiting in the same direction (pointing toward the bottom), and pass through the immediately adjacent 11°, now on the first row **(figure 7)**.

6 Repeat, alternating between rows 1 and 2 around the bottom of the cab, until you reach the uppermost pearl, which serves as the imaginary dividing line. Secure and trim the thread.

figure 5

figure 6

figure 7

On Cue
pin

Testing the durability of a new foundation, I bezeled a slice of billiard ball left over from another project and experimented with different beads around it. Fortunately, I bead better than I play pool! I love the end result, and it is a quick way to try out some of the new techniques we have covered.

a

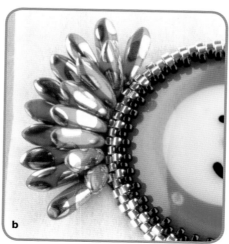

b

c

d

Materials

- 30mm round cabochon
- **5** 30mm bugle beads
- **5** 10x9mm Czech triangle drop beads
- **16–20** 10x3mm Czech glass peacock daggers
- **10–12** 7mm lentil beads
- **12–20** 3.4mm drops
- 1g 8º seed beads in **2** colors: A and B
- **10** 8º seed beads (to match triangle drops)
- 1g 11º cylinder beads
- 1g 11º seed beads
- 1g 15º seed beads
- Fireline, 8 lb. test
- pin back
- 4x5-in. piece of beading foundation
- 4x5-in. piece of Ultrasuede
- E6000 adhesive
- ½-in. wide Terrifically Tacky Tape

Tools

- beading needles, #12
- scissors
- embroidery scissors

Making the pin

1 Adhere the cabochon to the beading foundation using Terrifically Tacky Tape, thread a needle with a comfortable single-strand length of thread, and **bezel the cab (p. 17)**, starting with 11º cylinder beads and decreasing to 15º seed beads in a contrasting color. Once you have finished the bezel, secure and trim the thread.

2 To embellish the cabochon, think of your cab as a clock. Around the 9 o'clock position, stitch a **dagger row (p. 42)** of 10x3mm peacock daggers on the foundation, leaving a small gap between the daggers and your bezel **(photo a)**. Stitch a second row of daggers between the first row and the bezel **(photo b)**.

3 Add a 3.4mm drop **cluster (p. 21)** at the 11 o'clock position. Stitch tightly against the daggers and the bezel, and work out **(photo c)**.

4 Using stop stitch, add a lentil cluster at the 12 o'clock position, using 15ºs as **stop beads (p. 15)**. It should overlap the drop cluster slightly **(photo d)**.

5 From the 1 to 5 o'clock positions, **backstitch (p. 14)** a row of color A 8º seed beads tightly against the bezel, following the curve of the bezel **(photo e)**. Backstitch a second row of As tightly against the first row **(photo f)**.

e

f

g

6 Using stop stitch, add a cluster of color B 8º seed beads at the 7 o'clock position. Use 15ºs as stop beads. The cluster should extend slightly under the daggers and tightly against the bezel. For more depth and texture, add layers of 8ºs on top of the base layer of the cluster. Leave a ¼-in. gap at the 6 o'clock position **(photo g)**.

Finishing

1 Cut around your design as closely as possible without cutting any threads. Trim under the daggers so they extend beyond the foundation, and cut away the foundation at the ¼-in. gap **(photo h)**.

2 Test the fit of the Ultrasuede on the back of the cabochon. Identify where you want your pin back to be placed.

3 Finish with a **pin back (p. 33)**.

4 Edge your work with **blanket stitch edging (p. 26)** using 11º seed beads. Note that the edging is sewn under the cluster of daggers but around the other

h

embellishments, including the ¼-in. gap. When the edging is complete, knot the thread inside the beadwork/Ultrasuede sandwich, and trim.

5 To attach fringe, start a thread hidden inside the B bead cluster, and bring it up into the bezel. Working off the bezel, fill

the gap with five strands of **bail-ended fringe (p. 28)** as follows: the 11º that matches the drop bead, a 30mm bugle, an 11º, enough 15ºs to cover the thread, a triangle drop bead, and the same number of 15ºs used before the dangle. Secure and trim the thread.

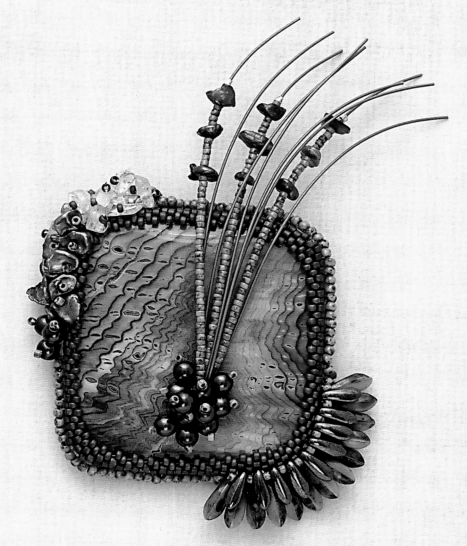

Unleashed
pin

Several years ago, jewelry artist Laura McCabe sent me a beautiful crazy lace agate cabochon with a drusy void near the center. I took one look at the cabochon and just knew that it had to become a pin/brooch with a cluster of beads exploding out of the void. It starts with a cabochon with a hole in it—either a void created by Mother Nature or one created by humans. If you have a hard time finding this type of cab, consider using a donut instead.

Materials

- 45–50mm cabochon with a hole or void
- **12–16** 10x3mm daggers
- **20–40** 4–7mm keishi cornflake pearls
- **10–12** 9x3mm "baby" daggers
- **10–20** 4–6mm gemstone chips
- **10–20** 4mm round pearls
- 1g 11º cylinder beads
- 1g 15º seed beads in **2** colors
- Fireline, 8 lb. test
- piece of beading foundation that allows at least a 1½-in. margin on all sides
- 1-in. wide Terrifically Tacky Tape
- 1 yd. 49-strand, .019 diameter beading wire
- 3x1mm crimp tube (**not** a size 3 crimp tube)
- **3** or more 1x1mm micro crimp tubes
- pin back
- Ultrasuede

Tools

- beading needles, #12
- crimping pliers
- scissors
- E6000 adhesive

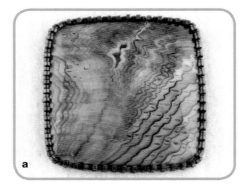

a

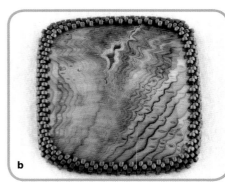

b

c

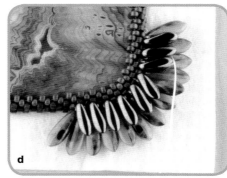

d

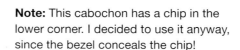

e

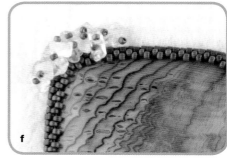

f

Creating the base

1 Thread a needle with a comfortable single-strand length of thread, and **bezel the cabochon (p. 17)** to the beading foundation. Start with an 11º cylinder bead, and decrease to a 15º seed bead. The number of rows needed will be determined by the height of your cab, the size of your beads, and the tension of your work. Once you have finished the bezel, secure and trim the thread **(photos a and b)**.

Note: This cabochon has a chip in the lower corner. I decided to use it anyway, since the bezel conceals the chip!

2 Decide which direction your cab will be oriented so that the spray will point in the angle you desire. The size, shape, and location of the void will be a major factor in determining the direction of your spray.

3 Line up 12 10x3mm daggers in a **dagger row (p. 42)** around the lower right corner of the cab **(photo c)**. Line up nine baby daggers on top of the first

row of daggers by **stitching in the ditch (p. 19)** in the peyote bezel just above your first row of daggers **(photo d)**. Pass through the bezel to turn your thread around, pick up an 11º seed bead, and pass through the first dagger. Stitch an 11º between each dagger. After the last dagger, pick up an 11º, and stitch into the bezel. Secure and trim the thread **(photo e)**.

4 Create a gemstone chip-and-15º **cluster (p. 21)** at the top left corner of the cab. Working around the corner,

g

h

i

j

continue to layer gem chips until you are satisfied with the cluster **(photo f)**.

5 Add a keishi pearl-and-15º cluster just below the gemstone chips at the top left corner of the cab.

6 Finish with a small group of 4mm pearls. Use the pearls in a cluster or a **pearl row (p. 47) (photo g)**. Cut around your design as close as possible without cutting any threads.

Creating the spray

1 Cut the beading wire into eight or nine strands approximately 3 in. long. Cut the tips of the wires at a slight angle. Slide the strands into the 3mm crimp tube. Make sure all of the strands are even on one side, and slide the crimp to the very edge of the cluster of strands **(photo h)**. Crimp securely **(photo i)**.

2 Embellish the spray next. Load a strand of beading wire with 15ºs until you reach the desired height of the first keishi pearl. Add a keishi pearl and at least one 15º to separate the pearls. Repeat as

desired **(photo j)**. Crimp the strand at the top of the last seed bead using a 1x1mm micro crimp tube. Be careful not to crush the 15º while crimping **(photo k)**. Trim the wire, if necessary. Repeat for each strand you wish to embellish.

3 To attach the spray to the cab, lay the spray in the void exactly where you want it positioned. Insert the crimp end of the spray into the hole **(photo l)**. (Depending on the depth and size of the void, you

may want to stitch a few 15ºs under one end of the crimp to support the spray at the desired angle.)

4 Start a new thread. Knot it on the back of the foundation, and bring it up through the void at about the position of the crimp. Working in and out of the void and weaving through the strands just above the crimp, secure the spray to the foundation **(photo m)**.

5 Embellish the opening with keishi pearls, round pearls, or gemstone chips with 15º stop beads. When the spray is secure and the hole is covered, knot the thread and trim **(photo n)**.

Finishing

1 Test the fit of the Ultrasuede on the back of the cab. Identify where you want your pin back to be placed. Finish with a **pin back (p. 33)**.

2 Edge the pin with **blanket stitch edging (p. 26)** using 11ºs. Note that the edging is sewn under the cluster of daggers but around the other embellishments.

TIP: To create the spray, I use 49-strand, .019 diameter Soft Flex beading wire, which is soft enough to move, stiff enough to stand up, and flexible enough not to kink. Lapidary Richard Alexis of The Art of Stone will cut voids into cabs for this project. Contact him at accurateinfo@aol.com.

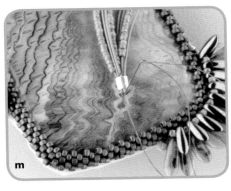

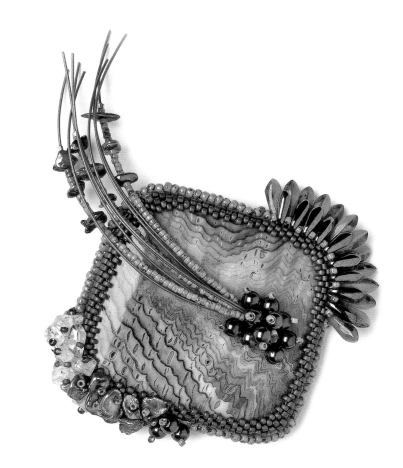

Spineless
earrings

These earrings feature fabulous pyritized ammonite cabochons. Ammonites are a group of marine animals that have been extinct for 65.5 million years. The shells of ammonites had hollow chambers separated by walls. Over time, pyrite, also known as fool's gold, enters the chambers, replacing the cellular structure cell by cell. Eventually, the ammonites are completely preserved in pyrite, giving them the appearance of being cast in bronze.

Materials

- **2** 30x25mm oval pyritized ammonite cabochons
- **16–20** 8x5mm Czech glass spikes
- **18–22** 3mm Swarovski pearls
- 1g 11º cylinder beads
- 1g 11º seed beads
- 1g 15º seed beads
- Fireline, 8 lb. test
- pair of glue-on earring posts with backs
- 4x5-in. piece of beading foundation
- 4x5-in. piece of Ultrasuede
- E6000 adhesive
- ½-in. wide Terrifically Tacky Tape

Tools

- beading needles, #12
- scissors
- embroidery scissors

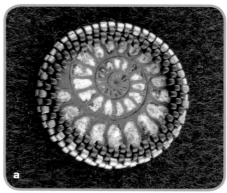

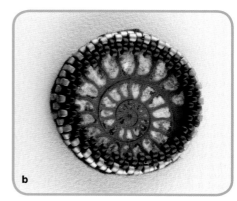

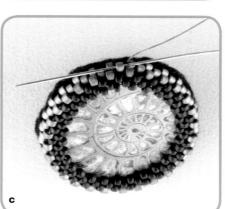

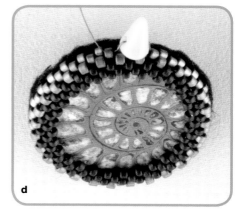

Making the earring

1 Thread a needle with a comfortable single-strand length of thread, and **bezel the cabochon (p. 17)** to the beading foundation. Start with 11º cylinder beads and decrease to 15º seed beads. The number of rows needed will be determined by the height of the cab, the size of the beads, and the tension of your work. Once you have finished the bezel, secure and trim the thread **(photo a)**.

2 Cut around the design as close as possible without cutting any threads **(photo b)**. Find the center of the very top and very bottom of the bezel. Start a new piece of thread, knot it, and pass through the beadwork to exit the top-center cylinder in the second row of the bezel **(photo c)**.

3 Add spikes by **stitching in the ditch (p. 19)**. Because of the size of the spikes, you will pass through every-other up-bead. Pick up a 8x5mm spike, skip over the next up-bead in the same row of the bezel, and pass through the third up-bead in the row **(photo d)**. Continue adding spikes in this manner until you have passed through the center cylinder at the very bottom of the bezel **(photo e)**.

4 With your thread exiting an up-bead in row 2, pass through the adjacent cylinder in the third row. To make the turn: Pass through the cylinder in row 1 that is directly below the bead you are exiting, with the needle pointing toward the spikes. Pass through the adjacent cylinder in row 2 **(photo f)**.

5 Pick up a 3mm pearl, and pass through the last spike you added **(photo g)**. Pick up a pearl and pass through the next spike. Continue until you have passed through the last spike.

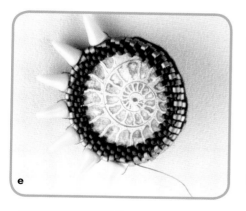

e

f

g

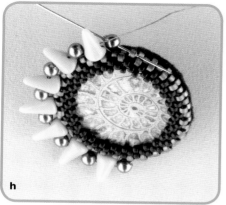

h

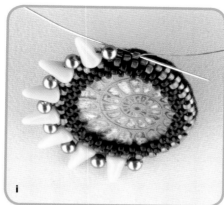

i

j

k

l

6 Pick up a pearl, skip the next up-bead, and pass through the following up-bead in the same row **(photo h)**. Pass through the adjacent cylinder in row 1 **(photo i)**. To make the turn: Pass through the cylinder in row 3 that is directly below the bead your thread is exiting, with the needle pointing toward the spikes **(photo j)**. Pass back through all the pearls and spikes. Pass through the center cylinder at the top of the bezel. Secure and trim the thread.

Finishing

1 Mark the vertical center of the cab. Apply E6000 adhesive to the entire back of the cab, and place the earring post on the back **(photo k)**.

2 Make a pinpoint hole in the Ultrasuede. While the glue is still wet, place the Ultrasuede on the back of the cab, pushing the earring post through the pinpoint hole. Press firmly so the backing is adhered to the back of the cab **(photo l)**. Put the earring back on the post to help protect it, if you like.

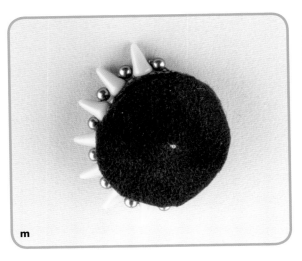

m

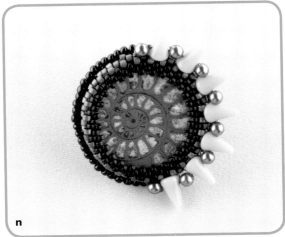

n

o

3 Trim the Ultrasuede to the size of the cab with the spikes protruding over the edge **(photo m)**. Edge the foundation/Ultrasuede sandwich with **blanket stitch edging (p. 26)** using 11º seed beads **(photo n)**. Secure the thread **(photo o)**.

4 Repeat for the other earring, making sure that the spikes are on the opposite side.

Iconic
earrings

I have always been fascinated by art deco architecture. I love the clean lines, geometric ornamentation and symmetry of design. Although I intended these earrings to be reminiscent of art deco architecture, fellow beaders have seen an Egyptian influence (they say the discovery of King Tut's tomb was a factor in the birth of art deco). Others have seen a pagoda. In either case, the secret to these lightweight earrings is the texture created by the blending of seed bead shapes, colors, and finishes.

Materials

- **2** 6mm metal rondelles
- **4** 5mm crystal pearls
- **4** 4–5mm button pearls
- 4mm bicone crystals
  4 color A
  8 color B
- 1g 1.5mm cube beads
- 1g 8º hex beads
- 1g 11º sharp triangle seed beads in each of **2** colors: A, B
- 2g 11º heavy metal seed beads
- 2g 11º seed beads
- 1g 13º Charlottes in each of **3** colors: C, D, E
- 1g 15º seed beads in each of **5** colors: F, G, H, I, J
- **36–40** 5mm silver bead caps
- **2** 3-in. 22-gauge silver headpins
- Fireline, 10 lb. test
- Fireline, 8 lb. test
- beading foundation
- Ultrasuede or other backing
- E6000 adhesive
- piece of cardstock

Tools

- beading needles, #12 and #13
- scissors and embroidery scissors
- chainnose pliers
- roundnose pliers
- flush cutters

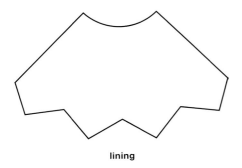

lining

a

c

b

Constructing the cone

1 Transfer the cone pattern to your beading foundation **(CD or pattern, p. 78) (photo a)**. Thread a needle with a comfortable length of thread, and knot the end.

2 Refer to **photo b**. Following the lines on the pattern, starting with the upper (narrowest) section on the top line and working down, **backstitch (p. 14)** as follows: a row of color J 15º seed beads, a row of color F 15º seed beads, a row of 1.5mm cube beads, and a row of 11º seed beads.

3 Using the **python technique (p. 22)**, add two rows of 8º hex beads secured with color G 15º seed beads.

4 Backstitch as follows: a row of 11ºs, a row of heavy metal 11º seed beads, a row of 11º triangle beads flush against the previous row, a row of heavy metal 11ºs (use this row of beads to encourage the triangles to stay in the proper position: point down, flat portion exposed), and a row of 5mm bead caps **stop stitched (p. 15)** with Js.

Tuck the tops of the bead caps under the heavy metal 11ºs, and make sure that the edges of the caps touch.

5 Move to the lower section to stitch the wavy lines. Starting at the bottom and following the curves, backstitch: a row of color C 13º Charlottes, a row of color D 13º Charlottes, a row of color E 13º Charlottes, a row of Ds, and a row of Cs.

6 Next, stitch the four large arches: Start at the left edge of the top line of the first arch. Following the curve of the arch, backstitch as follows: a row of Fs (the beads should slightly overlap the bead caps), a row of color H 15º seed beads, a row of Fs, and a row of Hs.

7 At the bottom of the arch, stop stitch a 4mm button pearl with a J. The pearl will partially cover the lowest row of the arch. Repeat on the other three arches.

8 Fill in the spandrels (the space between the shoulders of the adjoining arches): One of the four spandrels is split between the two sides of the pattern. You will work each half separately and connect them when you form the cone.

9 Backstitch a row of color I 15º seed beads on each spandrel. Fill in the open space on either side of this row arch with a single backstitched I. These beads will slightly overlap the silver bead caps above it.

10 Using stop stitch, sew a color A 4mm bicone crystal secured with a J

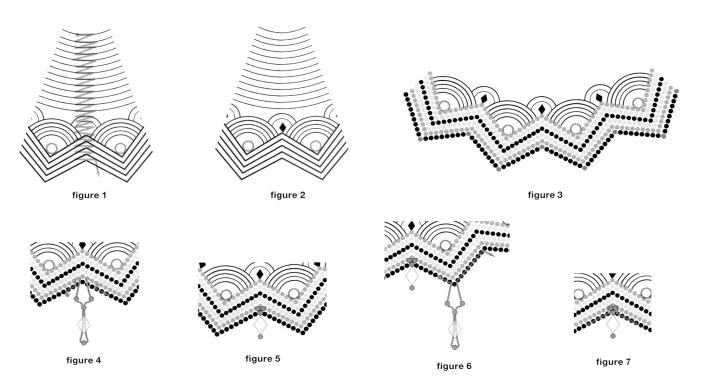

figure 1

figure 2

figure 3

figure 4

figure 5

figure 6

figure 7

at the lowest point of the center three spandrels. The bicone will partially cover the surrounding beads. (The bicone for the fourth spandrel will be added after the cone is formed.) Secure and trim your thread.

Finishing

1 Leaving a ⅛-in. margin on the bottom and both sides of the beadwork, carefully cut out the pattern. Trim the top only flush with the beads.

2 Thread a needle with a comfortable length of thread. Pull the long edges of the cutout together so that the rows of the pattern match up precisely. Bring your needle up from the back on the first row from the top on the left of the cone, approximately ⅛ in. from the edge. Bring your needle down through the first row of the right side of the cone ⅛ in. from the edge, making sure that your thread is hidden in the beads. Pull gently so that the rows match up and meet. (If you pull too hard, the cone will pucker.) Bring your needle up from the back on the next row on the left side of the cone ⅛ in. from the right edge. Bring your

needle down through the matching row of the right side ⅛ in. from the left edge. Pull gently so that the rows match up and meet. Repeat for each of the linear rows of the pattern **(figure 1)**.

3 Fill in any gaps in the rows with the appropriate bead. Using stop stitch, sew an A secured with a J in the center of the spandrel that was connected when the cone was formed. Secure and trim the thread **(figure 2)**.

4 Using the **lining** pattern, cut out a piece of lightweight cardstock (like an index card). Glue the cardstock to the Ultrasuede. Let dry. Trim the Ultrasuede to match the cardstock lining.

5 Roll the cardstock/Ultrasuede sandwich into a cone that will fit inside the earring cone with the Ultrasuede on the inside. Test the fit. Trim as needed **(photos d and e, p. 78)**.

6 Apply E6000 adhesive to the cardstock side of the inner cone, and slide it inside the beadwork cone. Make sure the lining

is completely inside the beadwork cone and that the points match up. If necessary, trim any exposed backing on the bottom and top of your beadwork sandwich.

7 Using **blanket stitch edging (p. 26)**, edge the bottom with Gs.

Making the fringe

1 When the bottom is completely trimmed, identify the center bead on the peak of each wave, and dip on the lowest wavy line (gold). The crystal drop is suspended over these beads **(figure 3)**.

2 Thread a needle with a comfortable length of thread, but do not knot. Bring the thread through a bead on the blanket stitch edging. Leave a 6-in. tail protruding from the bead you entered, which will be trimmed off later. Make a **half-hitch knot (p. 13)**. Pass through three more beads. Tie another half-hitch knot. Repeat. Trim the tail.

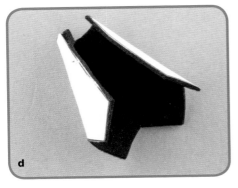

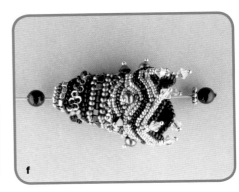

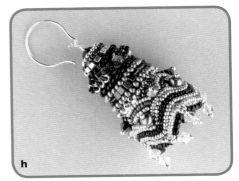

3 Pass the needle through the edge beads until you reach the peak of a wave. Move the thread up one row to the lowest wavy line so it is exiting the bead prior to the center bead. Pick up two Js, a color B 4mm bicone crystal, and a J. Slide the beads to the edge of the cone. Skip the last bead added, and pass back through the B and the second bead added. Pick up a J, and pass through the bead on the opposite side of the center bead on the wavy line. Pull firmly but not too tight **(figures 4 and 5, p. 77)**.

4 Pass through the blanket stitch edging until you reach the dip in the wave, and add a crystal dangle **(figures 6 and 7, p. 77)**. Repeat until you have a bicone dangle at the highest and lowest positions of each wave (a total of eight bicones).

5 Move the thread back to the edge beads and tie off the thread with several half-hitch knots. Trim the thread.

Assembly

1 String a 5mm crystal pearl and a 6mm metal rondelle on a 2-in. headpin. String the cone from the bottom. String a 5mm pearl on the headpin. The pearl should nestle slightly into the top of the cone **(photos f and g)**.

2 Create a wire-wrapped loop, and **attach an earring wire (p. 33) (photo h)**.

3 Repeat to make a second earring.

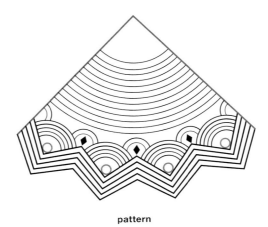

pattern

Other Side of the Moon
cuff

Decorative vase gems are unconventional—but completely wonderful—cabochon substitutes. Explore your bead stash to find colors that work with the stones, pick up a needle and thread, and let the beads do their thing. Layering many different types of beads and sewing others in dense clusters yields a fabulous texture. The result is an eye-catching bracelet using "cabochons" that literally cost pennies.

Materials

- **4 or 5** vase gems
- **10–25** 16x5mm daggers in **3** colors (solid, two-tone, matte AB, or peacock)
- **10–25** 10x3mm daggers (solid, two-tone, matte AB, or peacock)
- **25** 6mm Czech glass AB rondelles
- **12** 6mm fire-polished faceted rondelles
- **10–25** 6mm Czech lentil beads in **2** colors
- **15–20** 6x4mm Czech glass drops (or Magatamas)
- **10–25** Czech tadpoles
- **20** 4mm Czech druks, matte AB finish
- **25** 2.8mm Japanese drops in **3** colors
- 3g each of 11º round seed beads in **6–8** colors (a mixture of silver-lined, opaque, galvanized and silver-lined matte)
- 2g each of 15º round seed beads in **2–4** colors
- 2g each of 15º Charlottes in **2** colors
- Fireline, 8 lb. test
- foundation
- Ultrasuede
- **3** size 3 (large) hooks and eyes (round eyes)
- E6000 adhesive
- Terrifically Tacky Tape

Tools

- beading needles, #12 and #13
- scissors
- soft pencil (optional)

a

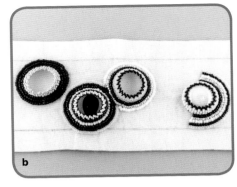

b

c

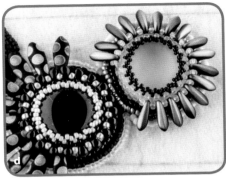

d

Making the cuff

Note: This cuff is 2 in. wide. Use the diagram provided on the CD or sketch a rough layout of your design on your foundation using a soft pencil. Allow for the inevitable shrinkage due to the density of the beads. Tailor your design to allow flexibility at the ends where you may have to add or delete for proper fit.

1 Using Terrifically Tacky Tape or E6000 adhesive, adhere the vase gem cabochon closest to the center of the bracelet in the desired location, and **bezel the cab (p. 17)** to the foundation. Start with an 11º seed bead, and finish with two or three rows of 15º seed beads or 15º Charlottes.

2 Repeat for the additional three cabochons **(photo a)**.

3 Before you embellish the cabs, **backstitch (p. 14)** rows of seed beads to cover the foundation around the bezel. Do some in all the same color, and try multi-color rings around the others. Once the cab is embellished with layers of beads, it is difficult to fill in under them. These beads will be mostly obscured by the layered beads, but this step will help prevent bare foundation from peeking through **(photo b)**.

4 Embellish the first cab: The last rows of the bezel should be 15ºs or Charlottes. Count down three rows from the last 15º row. **Stitch in the ditch (p. 19)** on this row of 11ºs to encircle half of the cab with a row of 16x5mm daggers.

5 After you stitch the last dagger, pick up an 11º, turn around, and pass back through the last dagger. Stitch an 11º between each dagger, and then pass through the 11º in the bezel immediately adjacent to the last dagger. Pick up an 11º, turn around, and pass back through the last dagger again. Pass through the row of daggers and 11ºs to reinforce.

6 To stabilize the daggers, embellish the row of 11ºs above them by stitching in the ditch with 3.4mm drops completely around the bezel. Connect the drops by stitching an 11º between each drop **(photo c)**.

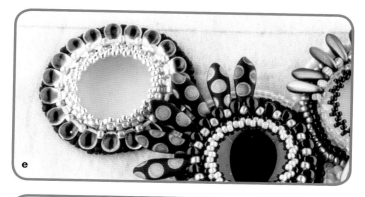

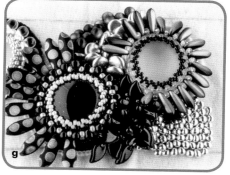

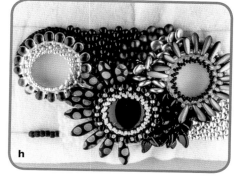

7 Work as in steps 4–6 to embellish another cabochon, but use 10x3mm daggers. Stitch an 11º between each dagger. Pass through the row of daggers and 11ºs several more times to stabilize and stiffen the daggers **(photo d)**.

8 Embellish the next cab with 6x4mm drop beads stabilized with 11º seed beads between each drop **(photo e)**.

9 Fill in between the cabochons with **clusters (p. 21)** of more daggers, small drops, tadpoles, 4mm druks, and lentils.

pattern (enlarge by 20 percent)

Using **stop stitch (p. 15)**, apply 6mm rondelles secured with 15⁰s or Charlottes in contrasting colors. Vary your colors and textures. Keep larger dagger clusters toward the center of the bracelet for wearability **(photos f–n)**.

10 Work multiple rows of backstitch using 11⁰s to outline the clusters. Vary the colors for contrast and interest **(photo o)**. When you are satisfied with your design, check for fit. Add more beads as necessary **(photo p)**.

Finishing

1 Apply backing (p. 25) to the bracelet. Edge your work with **blanket stitch edging (p. 26)** using 11⁰s.

2 Knot the thread inside the beadwork/Ultrasuede sandwich, and trim.

3 Attach hooks and eyes (p. 26) on each edge and in the center of the bracelet.

Take a Spin
cuff

My ophthalmologist is at one of the world's premiere eye hospitals, and I spend an interminable amount of time staring at that thingy with all those dials that they use to determine your prescription. On one visit, the dials fascinated me. I grabbed my sketch book (always with me) and started drawing. I knew my future focal had to move, and my solution was a repurposed binder post (also known as a Chicago screw) and a large eyelet. I love that the piece on top really spins!

Materials

- 10.54mm crystal rivoli, SS47*
- **10** 17x7mm Czech spikes
- **10** 4mm Czech glass pearls
- **175–200** 3mm Czech glass pearls
- 1g 11º cylinder beads
- 1g 11º seed beads
- 1g 15º seed beads (heavy metal)
- 1g 15º seed beads in **2** colors: A, B
- 1½ in. metal cuff
- Large eyelet set, ¼-in. (6mm) inside diameter, ⅜-in. (10.5mm) outside diameter
- metal Chicago screw set (also known as binder post) ¼-in. post length, ⅜-in. diameter head (available in office supply stores)
- E6000 adhesive
- 2x2 in. beading foundation
- 2x2 in. Ultrasuede
- 2x9 in. Ultrasuede
- fish leather to fit cuff blank
- G-S Hypo Cement
- Fireline, 8 lb. test

Note: The SS47 rivolis vary from 10.54–10.91mm in diameter.

Tools

- beading needles, #12 and #13
- scissors
- **2** eyelet tools
- hammer
- flexible tape measure
- permanent marker
- glovers needle or mini-pliers

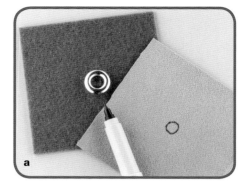

Beginning the cuff

1 Place the eyelet on the center of the beading foundation and trace the inside circle with a permanent marker. Repeat on the 2x2-in. piece of Ultrasuede **(photo a)**.

2 Carefully cut out the circle on both the beading foundation and Ultrasuede with a small embroidery scissors. Insert the top of the eyelet (deep half) into the hole in the foundation **(photo b)**. Do not glue the eyelet to the foundation. Use your non-dominant hand to hold it in place as you work.

3 Make a **dagger row (p. 42)** using (p. 42) 10 17x7mm spikes in a circle around the eyelet, with the wide end of the spike closest to the eyelet **(photo c)**.

4 Stitch a heavy metal 15º seed bead between each spike by passing through the holes in the spike.

5 Stitch a 4mm pearl immediately adjacent to each heavy metal 15º. Bring your thread up just below the heavy metal 15º, but touching the side of a spike. Pick up a 4mm pearl and pass the thread down on the opposite side of the pearl, touching the next spike. Bring the thread up on the other side of the spike just below the heavy metal 15º, but touching the side of the spike. Pick up a 4mm, and pass the thread down on the opposite side of the pearl, but touching the other side of the spike. Continue until you have stitched a 4mm between each spike. Pass through the first pearl again **(photo d)**.

6 To secure the spikes, create a loop of six color A 15º seed beads over each spike: Bring the thread out of one of the 4mms, string six 15ºs, and pass into the next 4mm. Make sure the string of beads sits on top of the spikes. Pull snug, but not too tight. Continue until you have a loop of 15ºs on top of each spike **(photo e)**. Pass through all of the loops and pearls again to reinforce. Secure and trim the thread.

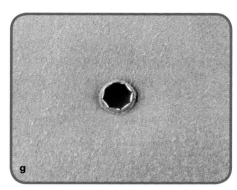

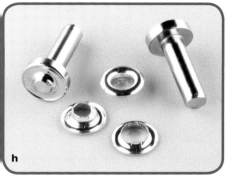

7 Cut around your design (along the 4mms and under the spikes) as close as possible without cutting any threads **(photo f)**. Remove the eyelet, and apply E6000 adhesive to the back of the beadwork. Place the 2x2-in. piece of Ultrasuede on the back of the beadwork, carefully matching up the center holes. Replace the eyelet **(photo g)**.

8 Trim the Ultrasuede to match the beading foundation.

9 Edge your work with **blanket stitch edging (p. 26)** using 11° seed beads. Secure the thread.

Attaching the eyelet

1 Gather your eyelet tools **(photo h)**. Have someone tightly support the mandrel circular base-side up resting on a firm surface. Insert the eyelet top (deep half) into the center hole of your beadwork from the top. From the back, place the shallow half of the eyelet over the center of the eyelet top **(photo i)**.

2 Position your beadwork (with the eyelet inserted) on the mandrel, bead-side up. Insert the second mandrel with the circular base side down into the eyelet center **(photo j)**. Make sure that everything lines up and the mandrel is not sitting on any beads. Hammer firmly

but gently. It just takes a few swings of the hammer for the center of the eyelet to split and secure it to your beadwork **(photo k)**.

Attaching the Chicago screw

The Chicago screw has two parts: the screw (the side with the grooves) and the post (the side with the open tube) **(photo l)**. Set the screw aside.

1 Cut a small circle of Ultrasuede to fit the top of the post (the flat part), and glue it on using E6000. Set it aside.

2 Cut two 10mm circles from your leftover beading foundation, and set them aside.

TIP: Craft stores sell eyelets/grommets in the sewing department (I chose the one made by Dritz). They usually come with a two-part grommet tool (not the pliers). It includes an anvil (a round disk with groves in it), and a mandrel (a long stem with a solid circular base). Unfortunately, if you use the anvil, you will smash your beads. My solution is to use two mandrels. You'll need a friend or family member who truly trusts you.

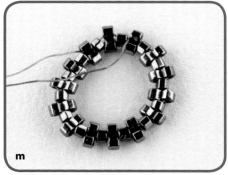

m

n

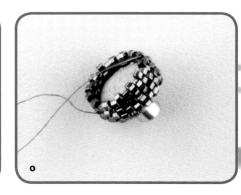

o

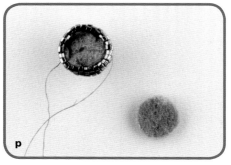

p

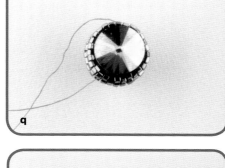

q

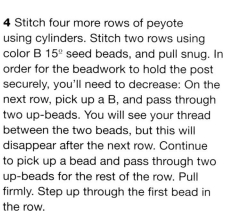

r

s

3 String 28 11º cylinder beads on a comfortable length of thread. Leaving an 8-in. tail, tie the beads in a ring using a square knot. Pass through one or two beads to hide your knot. Stitch a row of **even-count tubular peyote (p. 16)** using cylinders. You now have three rows of peyote (the initial string of beads become the first two rows when you add a third row) **(photo m)**.

4 Stitch four more rows of peyote using cylinders. Stitch two rows using color B 15º seed beads, and pull snug. In order for the beadwork to hold the post securely, you'll need to decrease: On the next row, pick up a B, and pass through two up-beads. You will see your thread between the two beads, but this will disappear after the next row. Continue to pick up a bead and pass through two up-beads for the rest of the row. Pull firmly. Step up through the first bead in the row.

5 For the next row, pick up a bead, and pass through the next up-bead (you will be passing over the pair of beads you skipped in the last row). Continue for the rest of the round. Pull firmly.

6 Pass through the beadwork to exit a first-round cylinder. Place the post into the beadwork with the flat top inside the peyote and the tubular portion protruding from the rows of 15ºs **(photo n)**. Turn the screw over **(photo o)**. Insert the two circles of beading foundation you cut earlier into the tube of beads on top of the post **(photo p)**. Place the rivoli on top of the circles of beading foundation inside the peyote column **(photo q)**.

7 Stitch two rows using Bs and one row using heavy metal 15º seed beads. If possible, pass through this row again to reinforce. The rivoli should now be securely encased in the beadwork **(photo r)**. Secure the threads and set aside.

Making the cuff

1 Using a tape measure, mark the exact center (horizontal and vertical) of your cuff with a permanent marker **(photo s)**.

2 Line (p. 25) the inside of your cuff with the 2x9-in. piece of Ultrasuede. Trim, leaving a ⅛-in. margin on all sides.

3 Test the fit of the fish leather on your cuff, and identify its approximate center.

Cut a tiny hole in the center of the fish leather just large enough to fit over the grooved stem of the screw portion (not the head) of the Chicago screw. The fish leather is very tough, so you may have to cut from both the front and back. Test the screw to be sure that it will pass through the hole easily.

4 Using G-S Hypo Cement, glue the screw portion of the Chicago screw on the center mark, grooved-side up. Let dry.

5 Carefully protecting the screw, apply E6000 to the top of the cuff, leaving a ⅛-in. margin to accommodate spreading **(photo t)**.

6 Position the hole you cut in the fish leather directly over the stem of the screw. Apply the fish leather to the top of the cuff, making sure that the entire top of the cuff is covered. Smooth out any wrinkles or air bubbles. Let it dry.

7 Trim the fish leather to the size of the Ultrasuede (the size of the cuff, plus a ⅛-in. margin on all sides) **(photo u)**. Edge with **blanket stitch edging (p. 26)** using 3mm pearls. Fish leather is extremely tough (and the back has a tendency to fray), so use a Glovers needle or mini-pliers to pull the needle through. Knot the thread inside the beadwork/Ultrasuede sandwich, and trim.

Assembly

1 Set the finished beadwork on the screw on the cuff **(photo v)**. Place a tiny dab of G-S Hypo Cement on the grooves of the Chicago screw on the cuff, making sure that none of the adhesive gets on your beadwork.

2 Working quickly, fit the embellished post on to the screw. Carefully grasping the peyote embellishment, gently twist it as tightly as you can. Let dry **(photo w)**.

Sakura
bracelet

One of my all-time favorite cuffs is a bit over-the-top in terms of wearability—so this is a scaled-down version of the original with many of the same elements. The piece was inspired by the central cabochon, which led me to use a pink foundation. You will note that in two areas I have allowed the foundation to show through. If you would prefer not to have the foundation show, replace the meandering ribbon of Tila beads with a wandering stream of bugle beads.

PATTERN ON CD

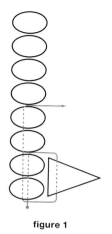

figure 1

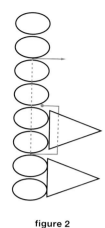

figure 2

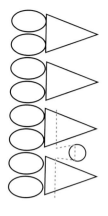

figure 3

Materials

- 40mm (approximately) irregularly shaped cabochon
- 10–12mm top-drilled oval pearl
- 16-in. strand 8–12mm branch beads
- 16-in. strand 6–8mm center-drilled cornflake keishi pearls
- 8x5mm Czech spikes
  12 color A
  4 color B
- 6x4mm Czech glass drops
  9 color A
  3 color B
- **15–20** Czech tadpoles in **2** colors
- **30–35** Rizo beads
- **40–50** 4mm Czech rounds or druks
- **20–25** Tila beads
- 5g 6º seed beads
- 5g 6º Charlottes
- 5g 8º seed beads in **2** colors*
- 10g 8º or 2.8mm drop beads in **2** colors*
- 10g 8º triangle seed beads
- 10g 8º hex seed beads in **2** colors*
- 10g 11º seed beads in **2** colors*
- 1g 11º cylinder beads
- 5g each of 15º seed beads or Charlottes in **3** contrasting colors
- clasp
- 4x9 in. beading foundation
- E6000 adhesive
- 4x9 in. Ultrasuede
- Fireline, 8 lb. test

Choose contrasting colors, one light and one dark.

Tools

- beading needles, #12 and #13
- scissors

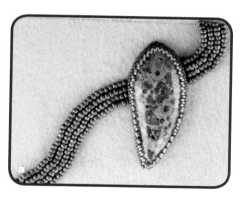

Beginning the bracelet

1 Transfer the bracelet pattern to your beading foundation **(CD or pattern, p. 91)**.

2 Thread a needle with a comfortable single-strand length of thread, and **bezel the cabochon (p. 17)** to the beading foundation. Start with an 11º cylinder bead and decrease to a 15º seed bead. The number of rows needed will be determined by the height of your cab, the size of your beads, and the tension of your work. Once you have finished the bezel, secure and trim the thread.

3 Start at the bottom margin to the left of the cab, and work toward the nearest edge of the cab about two-thirds from the bottom. **Backstitch (p. 15)** a curved four-row ribbon of 8º seed beads. Envision an imaginary line angled through the cab, and picked up on the other side. Continue the meandering ribbon all the way to the top margin to the right of the cab. Pass through the rows several times to reinforce, and zigzag between the rows to bind them together **(photo a)**.

4 Starting below the four-row ribbon and working down, find the second-highest cylinder bead row on the bezel. **Stitch in the ditch (p. 19)** with eight 6º seed beads.

5 Work your thread down to the foundation, and reinforce the beads by passing up through the foundation, through the 6ºs, and back down through the foundation.

6 Bring the thread up, and pass through two of the 6ºs. Pick up an 8x5mm spike, and pass back through the same two 6ºs in the same direction **(figure 1)**. Pass through the next two 6ºs. Repeat **(figure 2)** until you have four spike beads protruding horizontally from the edge.

7 Bring your thread up through the foundation, pass through the first spike bead, and pass down into the foundation to secure **(figure 3)**. Repeat for each spike.

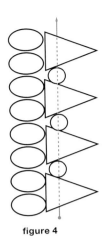

figure 4

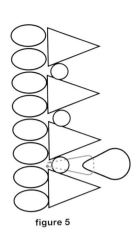

figure 5

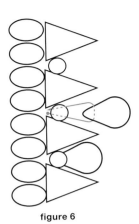

figure 6

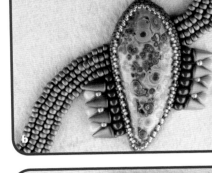

8 Bring your thread up through the foundation, pass through the first spike bead, pick up an 11º seed bead, and pass through the next spike. Pick up an 11º, and pass through the next spike. Repeat **(figure 4)**.

9 Bring your thread up through the foundation immediately against the bezel and between two spikes. Slide your needle under the 11º, pick up a 6x4mm drop, and pass back under the 11ºs, down through the spot you brought your thread up immediately against the bezel, and between two spikes **(figure 5)**. Pull snug so the point of the drop slides under the 11º and only the ball of the drop protrudes. Repeat **(figure 6)** to add a drop between each pair of spikes.

10 Repeat steps 4–9 to stitch an identical element on the opposite side of the cab just below the 8º bead ribbon **(photo b)**.

11 Directly above the cab, stop stitch a **cluster (p. 21)** of branch beads using matching 15ºs as a stop beads.

12 Starting at the lower margin to the left of the strip of backstitched 8ºs, stop stitch a four-row ribbon of 8º hex beads following the same path (use contrasting 15ºs as stop beads). The ribbon will be interrupted by the branch bead cluster and the top of the cab. Pick up on the opposite side, and continue to the margin.

13 Starting at the lower margin on both sides of the cab and working up and toward the outside, stop stitch meandering rows of 4mm rounds or druks, using contrasting 15ºs as stop beads. The path on the left will be interrupted by the ribbons of beads already stitched. Continue on the opposite side **(photo c)**.

14 Stitch a cluster of 8º or 2.8mm drop beads in the first color around the spike/drop element to the left of the cab, stopping at the ribbon of rounds. In the triangle between the 8º ribbon and the 4mm rounds, stitch a cluster of tadpole pendants, using contrasting 15ºs as stop beads.

15 To the right of the cab, create a waterfall effect by backstitching curved rows of 11ºs that match the color of the spike or drop it is emanating from—two rows for each drop and one row from each spike. The waterfall will be interrupted by the ribbon of 4mm rounds and continue to the margin.

16 In the space between the waterfall and the cab, stop stitch a cluster of 6–8mm cornflake keishi pearls with contrasting 15º stop beads.

17 Above the waterfall, stitch two four-row stop stitch ribbons that follow the curve of the original 8º ribbon and run to the upper margin. The first ribbon uses 8º triangle beads with contrasting 15º stop beads. The second (to the right) uses 8º hexes with contrasting 15º stop beads **(photo d)**.

18 At the upper margin to the right of the 8º hex ribbon, stitch a spike/drop combination as in steps 5–9, using the second color of spikes and drops. Fill in between this element and the ribbon of 4mm rounds with another cluster of stop stitched cornflake keishi pearls.

19 Stitch a small cluster of the second-color tadpole pendants using contrasting 15ºs as stop beads below the spike/drop element just added. In the space bordered by the 8º hexes, the

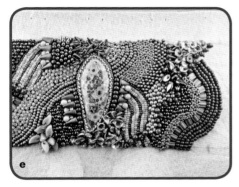

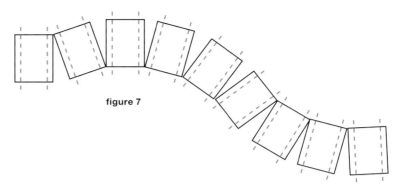

figure 7

tadpole cluster, the 4mm round ribbon, and the waterfall, stitch a cluster of second-color 8º or 2.8mm drop beads.

20 Starting at the base of the top-right keishi pearl cluster and to the right of the 4mm round ribbon, stitch a meandering ribbon of Tila beads. Bring your needle up through the foundation, pick up a Tila, and pass down into the foundation. (Notice that there is a top and a bottom on a Tila. Choose the side you like, and use it consistently in that direction.) Come back up, pass through the second hole of the Tila, and pass down into the foundation. Bring your needle up through the foundation immediately adjacent to the last Tila, and pick up a new Tila— but this time, angle the Tila, leaving a 2–3mm gap between the corners of the Tilas before passing back down into the foundation (note that your foundation will show through here). Come back up, pass through the second hole of the Tila, and pass down into the foundation. The placement of this gap determines the direction the ribbon will curve **(figure 7)**.

21 To the left of the Tila ribbon (following its curve), stitch a ribbon of 8º triangle beads with contrasting 15º stop beads.

22 Fill in between the strip of triangles and the ribbon of 4mm rounds with a cluster of first-color 8º or 2.8mm drops, extending all the way to the lower margin.

23 To the right of the Tila ribbon and following its curve, stitch a four-row strip of backstitched second-color 8ºs. At the intersection of the 8º strip and the 4mm rounds of druks, add the 10–12mm top-drilled oval pearl, and wrap it with two or three rows of backstitched 11º seed beads **(photo e)**.

pattern

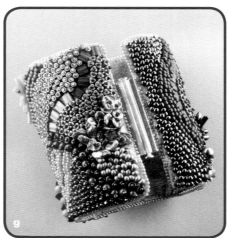

Finishing

1 Apply backing (p. 25) to your bracelet. Edge your work with **blanket stitch edging (p. 26)** using 11⁰s. Knot the thread inside the beadwork/Ultrasuede sandwich, and trim.

2 Add a multistrand clasp: Bring a new thread through a few edge beads several inches from where the clasp will be attached. Make a **half-hitch knot (p. 13)**. Working toward the clasp, pass through three more beads. Tie a half-hitch knot. Repeat. Center the clasp on the edge of the bracelet. Pass through the edging to reach the edge bead closest to the first ring on the clasp.

3 Pass through the first ring on the clasp from back to front. Pick up an 11⁰, and pass back through the ring. Skipping over the edge bead closest to the ring, pass through the next edge bead. Pull snug.

4 Pass through the second ring on the clasp from back to front. Pick up an 11⁰. Pass back through the ring. Skip an edge bead, and pass through the next edge bead. Repeat until you have stitched through all of the rings. Pass through two edge beads, and tie a half-hitch knot. Turn around and follow the thread path until you have reinforced each of the stitches. End the thread.

5 Repeat on the other end, making sure both halves of the clasp line up **(photos g and h)**.

24 To the right of the four-row stitch of second-color 8⁰s, start a cluster of first-color 8⁰ or 2.8mm drops.

25 On the left side of the bracelet, stitch a small cluster of Rizo beads to the left of the branch bead cluster. To the left of that, work a spike-drop combination as in steps 4–9 in the original color scheme, starting with a backstitched row of eight 6⁰s adjacent to the Rizos. Then stitch a waterfall element (as in step 15) emanating from the spike/drop combination, and end in the left 4mm round ribbon. Fill in between the waterfall, the top margin, and the uppermost section of the 4mm round ribbon with a cluster of stop stitched first-color 8⁰ hex beads, using matching 15⁰ stop beads.

26 To the left of the 4mm round ribbon, stop stitch a strip of 6⁰ Charlottes with 15⁰ stop beads that follow the same path. Below that to the left of the original hex ribbon, stitch a second meandering strip of Tilas extending all the way to the margin. Below that, to the left of the Tilas, stop another four-row strip of 8⁰ triangles with contrasting 15⁰s. In the "V" created by the 6⁰ Charlotte ribbon and the strip of triangles, stop stitch another cluster of keishi pearls. Fill in above that with a cluster of second-color 8⁰ or 2.8mm drops.

27 Test the fit of the bracelet, allowing space for the clasp. Extend the clusters of beads on either end of the bracelet to adjust for size **(photo f)**.

Radiator Road
collar

These amazing 30mm matte gold bugles inspired the "radiator" pattern in this collar. Tierracast pewter bead bars and links also work for this pattern, and my instructions explain how to apply them. If you are not locked into the gold color, use any 30mm bugle bead (you'll need an 11º seed bead at each end to prevent the rough edges from cutting the thread).

Materials

- **3** 20mm vintage brass bead caps
- 16mm Swarovski margarita
- **2** 14mm Swarovski margaritas
- **25** 1¼-in. bead bar connectors (TierraCast) or 30mm bugle beads
- **2** 13mm crystal briolettes
- **30–35** 11mm (size 5) bugle beads
- **25** 16x5mm Czech daggers
- **45** 8mm Swarovski margarita crystals
- **3** 8mm floral bead caps
- 10g 7mm Czech lentils
- **10** 6mm Swarovski margarita crystals in **2** colors: A, B
- **40** 6mm Czech glass rondelles or washers
- 16-in. strand 4–5mm dyed pearls
- **6** 4mm Swarovski bicone crystals
- **200** 3mm fire-polished round beads
- 5g 8º hex seed beads
- 10g 8º seed beads
- 20g 8º or 2.8mm drop beads in color A
- 10g each of 8º or 2.8mm drop beads in **2** colors (B, C)
- 2g 11º seed beads
- 10g each of 15º seed beads in **3** colors
- 8 in. sturdy chain
- **3** 15mm textured oval metal drops
- large S-hook
- **4–5** 3–4mm jump rings
- **3** 2-in. headpins
- beading foundation
- Ultrasuede or other backing
- Fireline, 8 lb. test
- E6000 adhesive

Tools

- beading needles, #12 and #13
- scissors
- chainnose pliers
- roundnose pliers

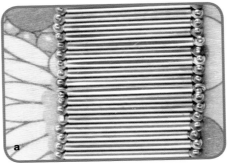

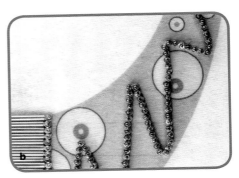

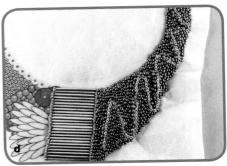

Making the collar

1 Transfer the pattern to your beading foundation **(CD or pattern, p. 97)**.

2 Starting at the bottom, stitch bead bar connectors or bugle beads, one immediately above the next, until you have filled the entire center space. If you use bugle beads, see p. 39. If you use connectors, apply them using **stop stitch (p. 15)**. Bring your thread up through the foundation exactly where you want the connector to sit. Pass through the ring on one side of the connector and pick up a 15º seed bead. Skip the 15º, and pass back down through the foundation in the same place you brought your needle up. Move to the other side of the connector, and repeat. Repeat for each connector **(photo a)**.

3 Stop stitch an undulating wave of 8º hex beads up the right side of the collar using 15ºs as stop beads, ending approximately 3 in. from the end. As the collar tapers, the wave will become smaller **(photo b)**.

4 Following the hex bead wave, **backstitch (p. 14)** 3mm fire-polished beads against each hex **(photo c)**.

5 Starting inside the waves and working out, fill in around the wave with a **cluster (p. 21)** of color A 8º or 2.8mm drop beads **(photo d)**. Bring the A cluster up to the bugle beads or over the right edges of the connecters to hide your stitches. Don't be concerned if there is a small amount of puckering with your foundation in this area. It is inevitable with a tight cluster of drops.

6 Following the pattern, stitch a vertical block of 30–35 11mm bugle beads curving up the top of the right side of the collar. Use an 11º as a buffer bead on each side to prevent the bugles from cutting the thread. Fill in around the bugles with a cluster of color B 8º or 2.8mm drops **(photo e)**. There is less wear and tear on your crystals if you apply them at the end, so move to the other side of the collar.

7 Stitch a three-row 16x5mm **dagger cluster (p. 42)** to the left of the bugles/connectors at the bottom. Backstitch a row of seven daggers.

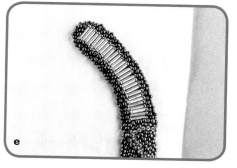

e

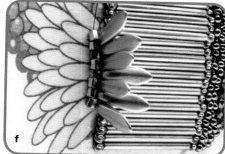

f

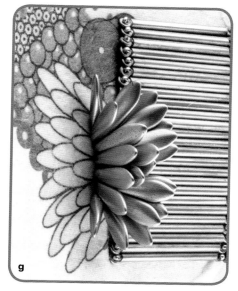

g

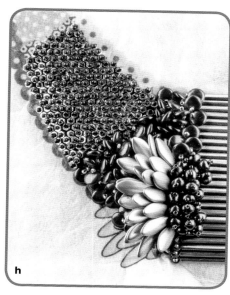

h

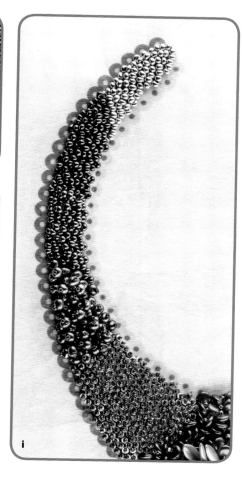

i

8 Backstitch a row of eight hexes tightly against the back of the daggers for support **(photo f)**.

9 To stitch a row of eight daggers on top of the hexes, bring the thread out of an end hex, pass through a dagger, and then pass back through the hex from the other side. Pass back through the dagger. The dagger is now sitting on top of the hex. Pick up a dagger and stitch through the second hex from the far side toward the dagger you just added. Pass through the dagger in the original direction again. Repeat to add six more daggers. Pass down through the foundation and come back up. Stitch through all eight daggers to reinforce.

10 Backstitch another row of seven daggers tightly against the second row **(photo g)**.

11 Stitch a 4–5mm **pearl cluster (p. 47)** (using 15°s as stop beads) next to the dagger cluster to hide the base of the daggers. Allow it to extend over the top of the neighboring bugles/connectors to hide those stitches.

12 Above the dagger cluster, stitch a **lentil cluster (p. 45)** using 15°s as stop beads. Extend it behind the dagger cluster (work tightly against the back of the dagger cluster to help the daggers stand up), and allow it to extend over the top of the neighboring bugles/connectors to hide the stitches.

13 Stitch a block of hexes using **python technique (p. 22)**, with 15°s as stop beads **(photo h)**.

14 Transition into another matching pearl cluster. After about 1 in., contour it toward the outside edge of the collar as shown in the pattern.

15 Following the contours as shown, stitch 8° or 2.8mm drop clusters in blocks of colors A, B, and C **(photo i)**.

16 Starting at the bugles/connectors and working toward the end, stop stitch a row of 6mm washers (or rondelles) along the entire inside edge of the left side of the collar. Use 15°s as stop beads.

j

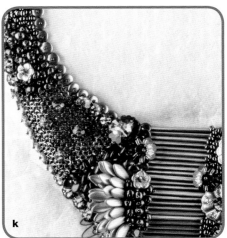

k

l

m

n

17 Starting at the bugles/connectors and working towards the end, stop stitch a row of 8mm margaritas along the entire outside edge of the color. Use 15°s as stop beads. You will have to stitch the margaritas along the edge and under the dagger cluster **(photo j)**. Warning: the margaritas will cut your thread. Use Fireline and make sure you always pull away from the margarita and not against one of the edges.

18 Embellish your work using stop stitch with 6mm, 14mm, and 16mm color A margaritas with 15° stop beads, and 8mm floral bead caps with 4mm crystal and 15° stop beads. Using **stack stitch (p. 16)**, layer 20mm bead caps with 6mm margaritas and 15° stop beads. Top the python section of hexes with a few color B 6mm margaritas **(photo k)**.

Finishing

19 Apply backing (p. 25) to your collar. When trimming your foundation along the left side of the collar, carefully cut the foundation away so that the outside edge of the 8mm margaritas and 6mm rondelles protrude from the edge.

20 Use a **blanket stitch edging (p. 26)** with 8° seed beads. If the edge beads at the top of your center bugle/connector block refuse to cooperate, use a tiny amount of E6000 adhesive to carefully glue the edge beads to the top bugle/connector.

21 You have many choices for a closure. For this example, I have chosen the collar chain clasp. Divide your sturdy

chain into two sections. One length should be approximately the length of the distance from the edge of the collar to the center of the neck. The other side can be as long as you choose.

22 Find the center edge bead at the end of your collar. Bring your needle out of the edge bead two beads before the center, facing toward the middle. Pick up six 15°s and an end link of the short chain, and pass back through the edge bead two beads after the center. Pass through a few beads, tie a **half-hitch knot (p. 13)**, and turn around. Reinforce your loop of 15°s as many times as you can comfortably pass your needle through. Repeat on the other end with the long chain.

23 Tightly secure a hook or S-hook to the short length of chain **(photos l and m)**. Your necklace can now be clasped by latching the open end of the hook to any link in the chain secured to the other edge of the necklace.

24 Embellish the chain with fringe, dangles, charms, or all of the above. I attached two 13mm crystal briolettes to the chain with jump rings, and created three dangles with 4mm bicone crystals on top of 15mm textured oval drops on 2-in. headpins **(photo n)**. When worn, the long chain will hang down the back of the neck.

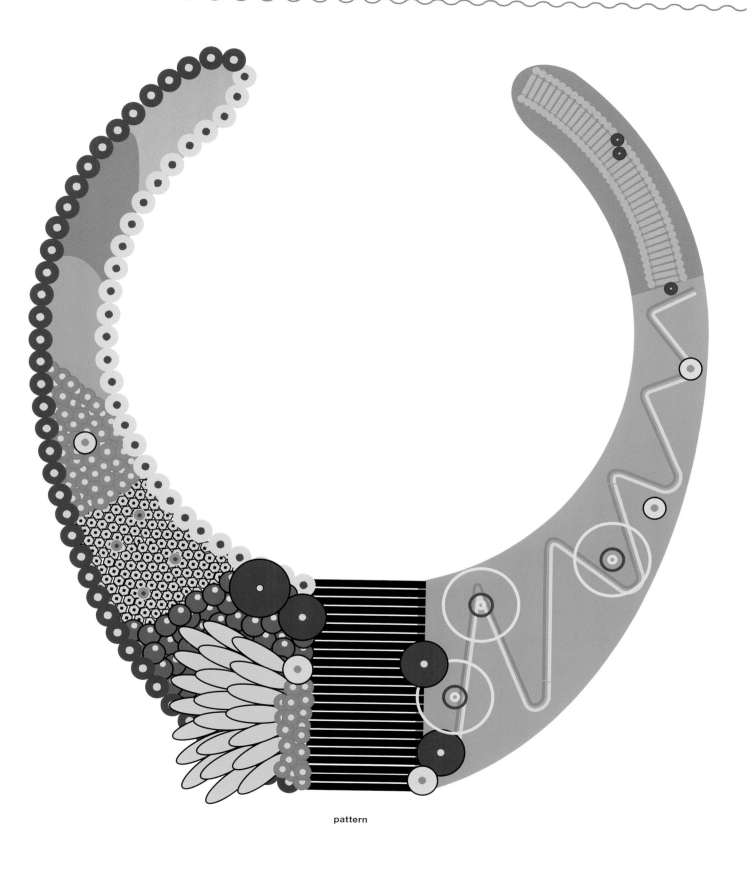

pattern

Pemaquid Sunset
collar

This collar is a study in flow. I used color to draw an imaginary line from the top right of the focal cabochon down to the left. The cascade of keishi pearls spills down until it hits the secondary cab. At that point, the stream widens and separates into two colors. Meanwhile, a trickle of metallic beads follows the same path to the right. It features many of my favorite bead embroidery techniques.

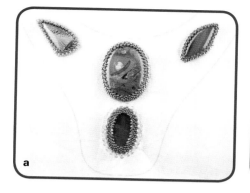

a

b

c

Making the collar

1 Transfer the pattern to the beading foundation **(CD or pattern, p. 102)**.

2 Refer to the pattern for placement of the four cabochons: place a central focal, a right, a left, and a bottom cab. Place the focal cab (the largest) in the center of the collar, ½ in. from the neckline edge. Place the other three 1 in. from the focal in each direction. The bottom should be centered on the focal. The left and right cabs should be positioned so that their midpoint is in line with the top of the focal cab. Trace around the cabochons, and set them aside.

3 Adhere the focal cab to the beading foundation using Terrifically Tacky Tape, thread a #12 needle with a comfortable single-strand length of thread, and **bezel the cab (p. 17)**, starting with an 11º seed bead and decreasing to a 15º seed bead. The number of rows needed will be determined by the height of your cab, the size of your beads, and the tension of your work.

4 Repeat step 2 with the remaining three cabs using different color combinations of 11º and 15ºs **(photo a)**. Embellish

the cabs, if desired **(photo b)**. Once you have finished the bezel, secure and trim the thread.

5 Starting at the top left of the right cabochon and working toward the lower right edge of the bottom cab, stitch a ribbon of **mermaid tail (p. 48)** using cornflake keishi pearls with a 15ºs as stop beads **(photo c)**.

6 Starting under the right cab and following the edge of the mermaid tail diagonal (toward the right edge of the bottom cab), stitch a ribbon of **python technique (p. 22)** using 6º triangle beads with 15ºs as stop beads.

7 Around the lower edge of the bottom cab, stitch a patch of **cobblestone (p. 34)** using 6º seed beads with 11º as stop beads. Fill in any open spaces where a 6º will not fit with an 8º hex bead.

Materials

- 40mm stone donut
- 30x40mm cabochon
- **3** 20–30mm irregularly shaped cabochons
- 15mm drilled unpolished gemstone nugget
- **2** 16-in. strand 8–12mm gemstone chips
- 16-in. strand 8–10mm center-drilled cornflake keishi pearls
- 8mm round gemstone bead
- **5** 6mm round gemstone beads
- 16-in. strand 12mm irregularly shaped gemstone briolettes
- 16-in. strand 4–6mm gemstone chips
- 10g 3.4mm drop beads in each of **2** colors: A, B
- 16-in. strand 3–4mm Czech crystal pearls
- 10g 2.8mm drop beads
- 5g Tila beads
- 10g 6º seed beads
- 10g 6º triangle seed beads
- 10g 8º hex seed beads
- 10g 11º seed beads in **4** colors
- 5g each of 15º seed beads or Charlottes in **4** colors
- **5** 20mm metal bead caps
- 2-in. headpin
- **2** S-hook clasps with jump ring
- beading foundation
- Ultrasuede or other backing
- Fireline, 8 lb. test
- E6000 adhesive

Tools

- beading needles, #12 and #13
- scissors
- chainnose pliers
- roundnose pliers
- flush cutters

8 Starting under the focal cab and running along the left side of the bottom cab, stitch a strip of clustered color A 3.4mm drops **(photo d)**.

9 Starting at the lower left corner of the focal cab, following the diagonal, stitch a **pearl cluster (p. 47)** of 3–4mm pearls using 15°s as stop beads. Continue the cluster of pearls above the top right of the focal cab, working toward the inside edge of the collar.

10 Work as in step 5 to continue the mermaid tail around the lower portion of the top right cab.

11 Move to the neckline above the focal cab and stitch a **cluster (p. 21)** of 2.8mm drops.

12 Above the upper right cab, stitch a cluster of 3-4mm pearls. Along the right side of the upper right cab, fill in between the 3–4mm pearls and the mermaid tail extension with a cluster of irregularly shaped gemstone briolettes.

13 Moving to the right neckstrap of the collar, **backstitch (p. 14)** horizontal rows of 11°s, working three-quarters of the way up the right side of the neckline.

14 Using **stack stitch (p. 15)**, decorate the backstitch rows with evenly-spaced stack-stitched embellishments **(photo e)**. Start with a 20mm bead cap, and pick up a 6mm round and 15° stop beads.

15 Above the 11°s, backstitch about 1 in. of horizontal rows of 8° hex beads. Pass through the rows of beads several more times to straighten and connect. **Whipstitch (p. 21)** a vertical row of 11°s along the edges to hide the stitches in the hexes.

16 Stitch about 1 in. of gemstone chip cluster, using 15°s as stop beads, after the hex beads. Finish the top of the right side of the collar with concentric ovals of backstitched 11°s.

17 Moving to the left side of the collar, embellish the area between the focal cab and the upper left cab: Stitch a row of Tila beads connecting the focal and upper left cabs at the halfway point

between the inner and outer edges. Bring your needle up through the foundation, pick up a Tila, and pass down into the foundation. (Notice that there is a top and a bottom on a Tila. Choose the side you like, and use it consistently in that direction.) Come back up and pass through the second hole of the Tila. Bring your needle up through the foundation immediately adjacent to the bead, and repeat until you have filled the space. Reinforce the row by passing back and forth through the Tilas.

18 Below that, backstitch several rows of 11°s. Reinforce to straighten. Beneath that, stitch another row of Tilas **(photo f)**. Finish off the bottom with a cluster of 2.8mm drops.

19 Above the Tilas, add a cluster of 4–6mm gemstone chips. Stitch a cluster of 3–4mm pearls between the chips and the inside edge.

20 Above the left cab, stitch a cluster of gemstone chips. Below the cab, stitch a cluster of color A 3.4mm drops. Connect the two with a small cluster of color B 3.4mm drops.

21 Moving up the left side, backstitch 1 in. of horizontal rows of 11°s matching those on the right side. Using stack stitch, decorate the backstitch rows with a 20mm bead cap topped with a 6mm round and 15° stop bead **(photo g)**.

22 Move to the top of the left side of the collar and backstitch concentric ovals using 11°s **(photo h)**. Below that, backstitch approximately 1 in. of horizontal rows of metallic 8° hex beads. Pass through the rows of beads several more times to straighten and connect. **Whipstitch (p. 21)** a vertical row of 11°s along the edges to hide the stitches in the hexes.

23 Below that, backstitch about 1 in. of horizontal rows of 11°s. Embellish with an irregularly shaped gemstone nugget topped by a 3–4mm pearl and a 15°.

24 Fill in between the two backstitched bands of 11°s with an 8–10mm gemstone chip cluster using 15°s as stop beads, a few rows of **python technique (p. 22)** using 6° triangles with 15° stop beads, and a small cluster of color B 3.4mm drops.

Finishing

25 Apply backing (p. 25) to the collar. Use **brick stitch edging** with 11°s **(p. 26) (photo i)**.

26 Create a **bead sandwich clasp (p. 32)**: String a 6mm gemstone, a 20mm bead cap, a 40mm stone donut, and an 8mm gemstone round bead on a headpin **(photo j)**. Pull snug so the components fit tightly together. Make a 10mm wire-wrapped loop. **Attach an S hook (p. 32)** with a soldered jump ring to each side of the necklace. Secure one of the hooks to the loop on the bead sandwich, and close the hook so that it will not detach from the loop. Clasp the necklace by latching the remaining S hook to the loop **(photos k–o)**.

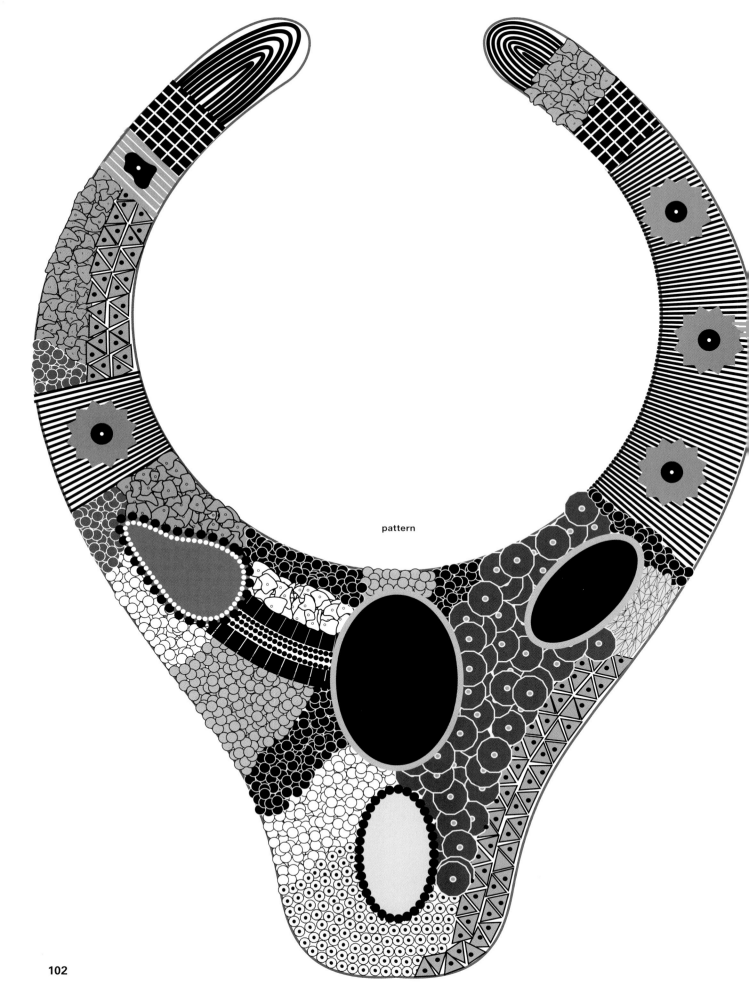

pattern

Personalize Your Pieces

Once you've practiced the techniques and made a few projects following my step-by-step instructions, you may be ready to design your own pieces. So, where do you begin?

INSPIRATION

Often a focal element will launch a new design, but you can find new ideas in many other ways.

Look for inspiration everywhere: color combinations in clothing, sheets, magazines, fabric, nature and—my favorite—articles and ads in in-flight magazines. Start an idea book with things that move you.

The advent of the cell phone camera has revolutionized capturing inspiration. You almost always have your cell phone with you ready to photograph things that inspire you. Keep a small sketchbook and make sure to sketch details and specific notes. I can't tell you how many times I have come across a design I sketched and have no recollection of what I was thinking.

DESIGN

Here is a general checklist of the process I use when starting a piece:

Inspiration: What inspired this piece? What "spoke to you"?

Elements: Were you moved by particular cabochon, a photo, something you saw, a special clasp, a tube of seed beads you couldn't live without four years ago, or maybe some great Czech glass?

Theme: Your pieces may tell a story. I've been inspired by a pinball machine, a frog in a marsh at sunset, and a trip down the yellow brick road to the Emerald City. How do you express a subject?

Drama: What can be done to make this piece unique and different? Think outside the box.

Style: Is there a particular style? Art deco, funk, retro, industrial etc.? Your materials should reflect this concept.

Color palette: What colors work with the key elements and theme?

Form: Is it a bracelet, earrings, necklace, or purse? What size?

FIT

Consider a few details before beginning a piece.

PATTERN ON CD

For example, how long do you want your bracelet? It is not enough to know the size of the wrist. A wider bracelet needs to be longer, and so does a thicker bracelet. A very wide cuff has to be contoured to accommodate the fact that the arm is narrow at the wrist and broadens as it moves up. Does your closure require an overlap? Will your clasp make the bracelet longer? All of these things need to be taken into consideration when starting a project.

Making a collar is even more complicated. You can't wait until you are finished to determine if the collar will fit. You need some basic measurements before you start.

How To Make a Collar Template

I originally learned how to fit a bead embroidered collar in classes with Sherry Serafini. She has a wonderful tutorial in her book with Heidi Kummli, *The Art of Bead Embroidery* (Kalmbach Publishing Co.).

I have included a collar template on the CD in the back of the book, but here are directions for you do-it-yourselfers. Enlarge, draw it on paper, cut it out, and try it on—if it does not fit, start over and adjust it to the size of your neck. Once you have found a proper fit, this is your starting template for future collars. If you plan to use it on a regular basis, laminate it or transfer it to a piece of cardstock.

1. Start by drawing a 5½-in. diameter circle. This is the inner edge of the collar.
2. Draw a vertical line through the center extending several inches below the circle.
3. Measure 1 in. down from the top of the circle on the centerline, and draw a horizontal line through the circle to identify the back edges. (Your clasp will add about 2 in.)
4. On each side, mark ½ in. outside the circle on the horizontal line. Call this side A and side B.
5. On the center line, measure 2 in. below the circle. Call this the front edge.
6. Draw curved lines connecting the front edge to side A and side B.
7. Fold the paper in half on the centerline to check to see if the template is even on both sides.

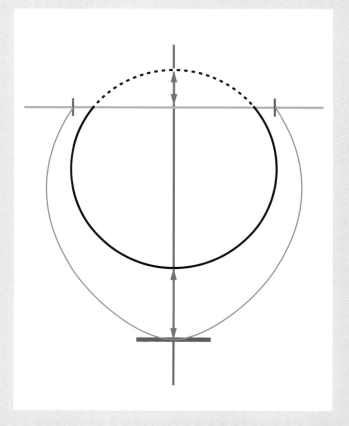

You now have your starting template for future collars. When designing a collar, start by tracing the inner circle and outside top edges of the template with a pencil. Then draw your design. Extend the edges to accommodate your components. Adjust the shape to make it interesting.

LAYOUT

I use two different processes to lay out a project, depending on the inspiration source.

If the elements are the stimulus, gather the focal components and most-remarkable beads. Lay them out on your work surface. Move them around until you are happy with the general layout—often, this step leads to the overall form of the piece. Play with as much detail as you like. Take a quick photo of the design and print it out. That's your blueprint. If you have been inspired by an idea or theme, sketch a rough design before you start. Include as much detail as you can. Determine what components you need to make the design work.

Regardless of the process, beads often have a mind of their own. Your initial design may not work, but the beads may lead you to something better. There are several factors you should address when planning a new piece.

Closure

You have a wide selection of options for finishing your piece, but it is best to decide before you start your work. For example, your choice of clasp will greatly affect the placement of beads at the ends of your design.

Flexible Design

When planning your design, keep in mind that the density of this style of bead embroidery may cause your foundation to contract. In order to prevent problems later, start working at the center and work out in each direction. Plan a design that is flexible enough to add more beads at the edges to compensate for the shrinkage.

Location, Location, Location

Don't place a major element on the underside of a bracelet where it will never be seen.

Weighting

Is your bracelet or pin properly weighted? You don't want it to spin on your wrist or look top-heavy.

Wearability

Pay close attention to how the wearer will be moving and any stress that will be put on the piece. If at all possible, the beadwork should move with the body; avoid anything that that would result in the jewelry breaking, bending, or sagging.

Comfort

The piece should be comfortable and drape well. That means no stiffness, scratchy edges, or components that flip or get stuck out of place. Collars should be tapered toward the back of the neck to lie flat. Are the protrusions on the bracelet going to catch on everything you wear? Do these beads make the necklace too clunky? Are those earrings too heavy to wear?

Scale

Is this too big for the average person to wear? Is the bracelet too wide? Are the focal components too small or large?

Design Guidelines

To create a good design, it is important to have a flexible but well-considered idea of the elements you will be using and general plan for their arrangement and use. These design concepts are most important in textured bead embroidery.

Color

Your choice of colors will have the greatest impact on a viewer's interest. My theme or focal beads (cabs, etc.) establish my color palette. "Desert River" (below) started with a fabulous Sonoran Sunset (chrysocolla cuprite) cabochon. The colors I chose faithfully mimicked the many tones in the stone—with a flash of neutral silver to add interest.

An effective color technique my mother taught me early in my beading experience is "puddling." Gather the beads you think might work and place them together in a big "puddle." Step back and look carefully. If a color is wrong, it will stand out like a sore thumb. Remove it and step back again. Repeat. My mother insists that every palette needs an "ugly" color— an unexpected shade that is not a traditional hue in a color scheme. It's your accent mark, and it can give life to a project.

HARMONY

Harmony is the visually satisfying effect of combining similar, related elements to produce a more attractive whole.

The composition is complex, but everything appears to fit with everything else. No individual part is viewed as more important than the whole design. The whole is better than the sum of its parts.

You probably wouldn't pair rustic, chunky African beads with classic round ivory pearls. They just don't go together. But take those pretty pearls and group them with some glittering crystals, and you have harmony.

Emphasis (or dominance)

Emphasis is the part of the design that catches the viewer's attention first. The area could be different in size, color, texture, positioning, shape, etc. The focal point should dominate the design without sacrificing the unity of the whole. All of the other elements in the piece must work together to enhance and showcase your focal bead.

Contrast

A composition needs contrast because too much visual similarity becomes monotonous. Emphasize contrast to add excitement and energy to your work. Use contrasting colors. Position light beads against dark beads. Play with different finishes and materials. Combine smooth beads with faceted, irregular, or chunky beads. Place shiny metallics next to flat matte finishes.

Balance

In a nutshell, balance is how the placement of the elements within a piece satisfies the subconscious of the viewer. Think of an old-fashioned balance scale, such as the scales of justice. We know that if we put two identical items, one on each side of the scale, it will balance. That is called symmetrical balance—equal "weight" on equal sides of an imaginary center line (horizontal or vertical). Many bead artists do just that. One side of a necklace mirrors the other side of the necklace. It always works.

But sometimes, we feel the need to rebel. We don't always want both sides of the necklace to be exactly the same. Your work can be asymmetrical, but if it doesn't "balance," it disturbs the viewer and detracts from the work. Let's imagine that we put one big element on one side of our scale. We can make it balance by putting several smaller items on the other side of the scale. Seems simple, right?

Not so fast. Balance is not only achieved by size. Many different factors can give an element visual "weight." You can use color (the darker the shape, the heavier it appears), texture, patterns, novelty, and many other factors to achieve balance. A large element near the center can be balanced by a small one close to the edge. A large, light-colored element can be balanced by a small, dark shape. To further complicate matters, balance is affected by color in more ways than color intensity. My general rule of thumb is to make sure that every color in the palette is represented in some way on each side of a piece.

Proportion

Proportion is defined as "harmonious relation of parts to each other or to the whole." Keep the concept of proportion in mind when designing your work. When starting a bezel, coordinate the size of the seed beads to the size of the cabochon. Don't overwhelm your cab with extremely large embellishments. Don't finish a large bold necklace with a small lobster clasp. Don't use a tiny, insignificant focal on a large collar. You get the picture. It may take a little trial and error, but you will begin to master the art of proportion.

Flow or Movement

I consider "flow" to be a trademark of my style. Flow is the path the viewer's eye takes through the artwork directed along lines, shape, and color. A sense of movement is achieved through the arrangement of color, shape, size and through texture and pattern. Graduate the size of your beads. Transition your colors from dark to light. The movement within your art is what gives it life.

Interest

In beadwork, interest is the ability of the artist to make her jewelry unexpected, remarkable, compelling, and exciting. Variety makes your work interesting. If every bead was an 11° seed bead, your work would be very boring. Vary size, shape, and color to add texture and interest.

Drama is the primary goal in all of my beadwork—to create something that is startling and striking. Using items out of context highlights their physical properties (shape, color, texture, etc.) to evoke emotions, associations, and memories.

Interest and drama can be created by:
• Executing an obvious theme
• Incorporating unusual focal elements, bold color schemes, or unexpected components and materials
• Using unusual combinations of color and material
• Constructing a distinctive overall design (layout)

Although it is asymmetrical, this piece is balanced—colors A–E are found on both sides of the bracelet.

Notice the flow or movement of the piece—bead paths help the eye glide from left to right across the bracelet.

TEXTURE AND DIMENSION

The dictionary says that texture is the way a surface feels or is perceived to feel—rough, smooth, soft, hard, silky, pebbly, bumpy, and countless other adjectives.

In most mediums, visual texture is the impression of texture created by the artist's attempt to reproduce the color and value of real world textures. Visual texture is the illusion of having physical texture. Physical texture, also known as tactile texture, is the actual variations upon a surface. Unlike visual texture, it has a physical quality that can be felt by touch. When I talk about texture in bead embroidery, I am referring to a variation on both physical and virtual texture. Texture is an optical illusion that gives the work dimension and drama. It's the interplay of how each bead reflects light, to draw the eye to certain areas and let others recede into the background. It is the excitement the actual physical texture creates without the viewer ever touching the work.

"I am not the neatest beader on the planet. My work surface is usually strewn with all kinds of beads. I can't tell you how many times something on my table I would have never considered has worked its way into my color palette by chance. By the same token, tubes of beads rolling around in my tray at a bead show or store have gotten married without a proper introduction."

Maximize Texture
- Use beads that protrude beyond the level of your base layer of beads
- Emphasize color and finish contrasts
- Mix glossy and matte beads
- Use metallic beads—they work great in almost any project, as long as the color of the metal complements your palette
- Seek out beads and elements with variegated colors and interesting finishes
- Include beads with attention-grabbing shapes and coatings
- Use common beads in unusual orientations
- Incorporate found elements
- Cluster and layer your beads
- Embellish cabochons and other elements
- Vary the size of your beads, including the same color bead in multiple sizes

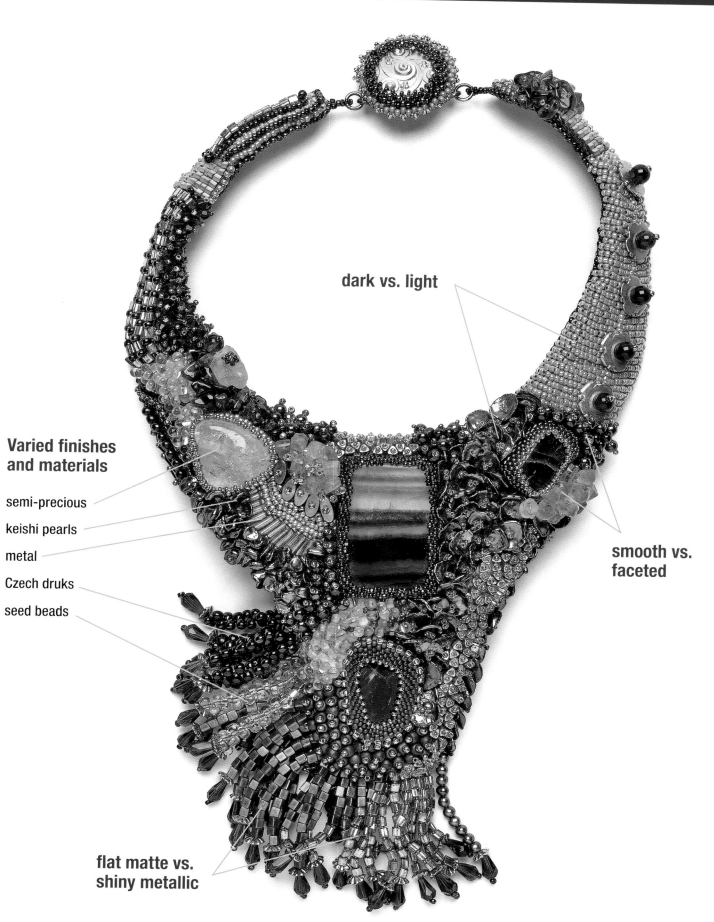

dark vs. light

Varied finishes
and materials

semi-precious

keishi pearls

metal

Czech druks

seed beads

smooth vs.
faceted

flat matte vs.
shiny metallic

UNITY

Last but not least, there is unity.

Unity is essentially the successful application of everything else we talked about in this chapter. When a design has unity, it will be viewed as a cohesive project rather than a bunch of unrelated elements. The edge of one element leads into another without distinct separation giving a sense of uninterrupted connection.

ACKNOWLEDGMENTS

Thank you to:

- My editor Erica Swanson for her vision and patience in making this book a reality.

- My husband Howard Landy for his photography skills, unwavering love and support, and willingness to eat Chinese delivery several days a week.

- My dear friends Katharina Keoughan, Gerry Shpiner, and Lynn Yuhr for encouraging (pushing) me to take the next step and emotional support every step of the way.

- My bead buddies Myriam Ribenboim and Susan Skor for helping with the beadwork (they are meticulous and much faster than I am...).

- My parents Howard and Natalie Kleinberg for surviving a series of orthopedic disasters perfectly timed to interfere with the writing of this book—and for a lifetime of love and support.

- My children Russell, Aaron, and Lisa for cheering me on, grandbaby Kayla (born two weeks after I signed the contract for this book) for keeping me from my work, and my constant companion Austin for sitting with me while I beaded into the wee hours of the night.

- The fabulous Sherry Serafini for inspiring me to become a bead embroidery artist, teaching me the basics, and writing the foreword for this book.

- Laura McCabe for her encouragement and for making me a better artist by sharing her incredible talent and attention to detail.

ABOUT THE AUTHOR

Linda Landy has been teaching beading in south Florida for more than 12 years. She also has taught at the Bead&Button Show, Best Bead Show Miami, and BeadFest Philadelphia. Linda won first prize in the finished jewelry division of Bead Dreams 2012 with a bead embroidered collar entitled "Tilt!" and was a 2010 Bead Dreams Finalist. She is a contributor to *Bead&Button* Magazine and *Beadwork* Magazine, and has projects in *The Big Book of Patterns* and *Creative Beading Vol. 7*.

Embrace the beauty of bead embroidery

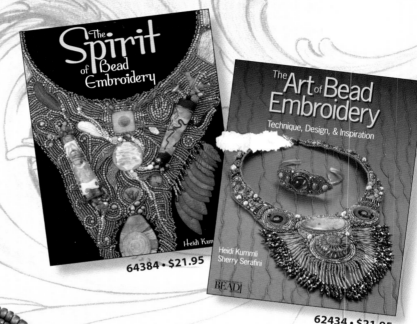

The Spirit of Bead Embroidery
64384 • $21.95

The Art of Bead Embroidery
Technique, Design, & Inspiration
Heidi Kummli
Sherry Serafini
62434 • $21.95

If you liked *Textured Bead Embroidery*, you'll love these projects, too!

Renowned artists Heidi Kummli and Sherry Serafini share their secrets for creating beautiful beadwork. *The Spirit of Bead Embroidery* guides you through 13 astonishing projects that reveal how the natural world can enhance your jewelry-making journey. In *The Art of Bead Embroidery* you'll find 12 gorgeous jewelry and ar pieces, along with inspiring design ideas.